WOMEN AND CHILDREN IN PROSTITUTION : HUMAN RIGHTS PERSPECTIVES

WOMEN AND CHILDREN IN PROSTITUTION :

HUMAN RIGHTS PERSPECTIVES

(Report of National Workshop)

Edited by

Madhu D. Joshi

A Joint Women's Programme Publication

UPPAL PUBLISHING HOUSE

NEW DELHI-110 002 (INDIA)

UPPAL PUBLISHING HOUSE
3, Ansari Road, Daryaganj, New Delhi-110002
Phones : *Off.* 3273756, 3286571 *Res.* 2242884

First Published 1997
ISBN 81-85565-76-7

Printed in India
Published by B.S. Uppal for Uppal Publishing House
3, Ansari Road, Daryaganj, New Delhi - 110002
Laser setting by Creative Lasertech, Paharganj, N.D.-55
and Printed at Arora Offset Press, Delhi-110092

INTRODUCTION TO THE WORKSHOP

This National Workshop on "Women and Children in Prostituion - Human Rights Perspectives" is being organised by the National Commission for Women and the Joint Women's Programme. This is the first time that we are trying to look at the problem of prostitution from the perspective of women's human rights. We are concerned about the growing instances of trafficking of girls into prostitution. We are also concerned about the voluntary entry of many women into prostitution because of poverty and lack of employment. Each one of us who is concerned about this issue has been trying to tackle the problem of prostitution in our own way but it has only increased with the opening up of markets to the internatonal arena, the increase in tourism and the globalization of media. Though more organisations have today taken up the cause of women who are exploited and forced into prostituion and there is an overall concern for justice for children and women trapped in this system. Many other types of sexual exploitation and abuse are becoming evident. One of the most dangerous being that which is supported by a nexus of pimps, politicians and police. The traditional forms of prostituion, specially those that were given acceptability by religion, continue, despite legislation against them.

Prostitution should be viewed in the context of the over all situation of the status of women in India. Old cultural and religious practices, superstitions, ill-teracy and patriarchy are generally responsible for the exploitation of women in every way, i.e. financially, psychologically and sexually. Prostitution, thus, is a symptom and not a malady. Thus the solution to the problem cannot be sought in isolation. Neither education of the women nor the eradication of poverty alone can actually change this situation. Besides, in India, most women and children come from that section of society, which is known as the scheduled caste and scheduled tribe. This vulnerable section of society being backward is exposed to brutality, abuse, mutilation, sexual exploitation and sale.

Migration, urbanisation and homelessness have led to the growth of prostitution. As industry has increased, communities which were free from prostitution, are also drawn into it. With the growth of tourism and abundant use of mass media and pornographic literature (which reflect the prevailing attitude towards women), more and more girls are being forced into this practice. Every city has cabarets, massage parlours, etc. to attract college girls looking for more money, who thus trapped into this system.

We need to expose and then destroy the mechanism through which women and children are trapped into prostituion. We need to remember that the majority of girls are forced into prostitution by unscrupulous people, poor parents and guardians, who do not mind selling their girl children, and other social pressures. Several of these women have been victims of rape, family violence, desertion, widowhood, etc. While framing suitable changes in the existing legislation, we need to remember that women alone cannot be blamed for this evil. It is society and its attitude towards women, the client who demands prostitutes, the procurers who kidnap and sell girls and the pimps who act as go betweens, who are to be blamed. Also the keepers of the law who fail to do their duty and the politicians who are either a party to such deals or silent, indifferent spectators, are equally liable.

Our action, therefore, needs to be not only in the realm of rescue and rehabilitative services, but also in preventive measures. It needs to consider prostitution from the point of view of violation of human rights, a hindrance to women's freedom, equality and struggle against exploitation and oppression.

This Workshop will, therefore, provide a platform for sharing of information, framing of concrete proposals and recommendations to be sent to the government, policy makers and voluntary organisations involved in work related to prostitution. It will enable us to evolve strategies that can be used at various levels to eradicate expolitation of women and children (girls as well as boys).

For us in the joint Women's Programme, it is our primary duty to :

1. Promote the self image of women;
2. Conscientise men about their role and status of women and the need to look at women as feeling, human persons like themselves.
3. Act as watch dogs in every area where we are working, in order to spot, check and help the police arresting those involved in trafficking;
4. Provide preventive measures;
5. Provide rehabilitation to women who wish to leave the profession.
6. Prevent children of prostitutes from being trapped into this profession.
7. Provide legal education and aid;
8. Organise health education programmes.

The aim of the workshop is to bring together like minded people to share and examine possiblities of securing justice ot these women.

It is also proposed to craft a monitoring mechanism to keep an eye on the system as it operates, as well as to identify areas and groups.

It is time we spoke out against the violence inflicted upon a woman in the form of sale of her body, the physical violence that is used to break her dignity, the violence in the form of denial of medical facilities and finally when she is left to suffer in old age and disease. It this is not violation of women's human rights, then what is?

Jyotsna Chatterji
Director - JWP

CONTENTS

1.
INAUGRAL SESSION

Smt. Mohini Giri, Chairperson, National Commission for Women

I welcome Ms. Krishna Sahi, our Union Minister, Mrs. Pramila Dandavate and other sister and women collegues with whom we are working and shall continue to work later on behalf of the National Cimmission for Women. I would like to state in the beginning itself that we have been sitting and discussing the problem in conferences and meetings for the last many years and yet we are not able to find a solution to the problem. Even if we are able to identify the problem, we are unable to solve it because of the problems that come before the Government or because of the lack of funds. or because of the obstacles caused by the transfer of the dynamic person who may have taken initiative in taking up that particular problem.

I hope that we will be able to take some decisions specially with regard to the children who are denied the facilities of education, a decent environment and find a solution to tackling their problems.

Recently I visited Bombay and I found that in the evening young girls who were barely eight or ten years' old were soliciting "Babu do rupya". Is this the culture of India?

With these words, I know request Jyotsna ji to explain the day's prodeedings.

Jyotsna Chatterjee, Director, Joint Women's Programme

We are indeed happy that all of you are here, but as you have heard Mrs. Giri speak just now our concern is not just to sit around the table and discuss the matter but to strategise on curtailing traffcking in women and girls into prostitution.

You all know that this matter is not something new. This is something that has gone on for ages and everybody gives us the excuse that this is an old custom and that it cannot be curtailed at all and that it is a necessary evil. We are told that because this practice is traditional we have to accept it and we a cannot root it out. We have to, however, understand the conditions that exist today. We have to work out a strategy so that we are able to change the condition that exist and find ways to rescue children and girls who get trapped in this vicious system.

At this moment we have just got in our hands some of the suggestions that have been made in the Platform for Action. At the recent International Conference of Women the question of exploitation of women and children in prostitution was discussed. Several of us have playing a major role in trying to make an impact on the policy makers to see how human rights questions concerning these women can be addressed.

With the opening up of the markets and globalisation of the media there is an increase in sex tourism.

While we share the common concerns, we need to recognise the various means by which trafficking is done. Where from these women get traffcked, who are responsible for trafficking, what are the mechanics, what is the role of politicians, the police and pimps who are involved in this process. We also need to recognise the various traditions and cultures that promote a certain type of prostitution that is given religious sanction. Once we are able to pinpoint the kinds of prostitution and the areas from which trafficking is done, we need to go on further to see what are the causes of the situation. Is it because of migration? Is it because if the lack of employment? It is because rural areas are becoming depleted of resources so that people have to migrate to cities? Or is it the patriarchal system system that is responsible?

We need to look at all these causes and go on further to strategise what are the problems these women are facing. Where are their human rights affected? In their daily lives, in their lack of facilities, in their lack of basic rights, in their health concerns, in their continuous struggle to exist, in the violence that is caused on them by their famalies, by pimps who are selling and buying them, by the madams who run the brothels, by the law and order machinery that continually tries to either promote trafficking or help in the trafficking.

Lastly we need to recognise that this problem cannot be curtailed or solved unless there is networking between the concerned organisations , the Government and the National Commission for Women.

I also feel that we need to consider what has been suggested as action for the Government. The Platform for Action has suggested certain measures to be taken by the Government of the countries form where they are bought and the destination that they reach.

1. We have to consider the ratification of the International Convention in Trafficking in Persons and on Slavery.

2. Second, to take appropriate measures to address the root causes including external fcators that encourage traffcking in women and girls for prostitution, forced marriages, labour; to eliminate trafficking with the view to provide better protection of the rights of women and girls; and to punish the perpetrators.

3. Three, set up measures and concerned action by relevant law enforcement machinery, authorities and institutions with the views to break the national and international network in trafficking.

4. Allocate resources to provide comprehensive programmes designed to heal vctims of trafficking, including job training, legal assistance and confidential health care , and take

measures to co-operate with the non-government organisations to provide for the social, medical and psychological care of the victims of trafficking.

5. Develop educational and training programmes and consider enacting legislation aimed at preventing sex tourism and trafficking, giving special emphasis to the protection of women and children.

We know that in many of our red light areas we have girls form across the borders. There are girls from Nepal, Bangladesh and we also know that there are girls going from within our countries to other countries crossing our borders. If we believe in human rights and justice we need to consider it and take a stand. we have to make a plan and take them to our area and see that it is implemented.

Smt. Krishna Sahi, Hon'ble Minister of State for Food & Civil Supplies

I am very happy to be with you today because I am getting this opportunity to address my dear women social workers after a very lonmg time.

Mohini ji has correctly stated that we have been discussion these problems for the last 30 years but I would like to point out that it is not only for the thirty years but since the last century we have been discussiong this problem. Today we are reaching for the stars and have made scientific and technological progress. Today women are coming out in larger numbers in all fields and even then women are are exploited by the system. I thank you for inviting me to this conference.

The topic of human rights is being discused in all fora. Today not only men and but also women are not mentally agreeable, to accept women in prostitution to be given any human dognity or rights. We have to give a thought to the women who may be working in prostitution because of certain compulsions, which may be either social or commercial.

There are two views about how one looks are women's body. Some look at it is as an art form and others look at it in a commercial form. In ancient days we had court dancers who enjoyed social status and respect but today women in this profession do not enjoy that respect or status. Commercialisation today has reduced such women to a commodity. I am happy that many women organisations have raised this point and are fighting against this commercialisation. women in modelling or in prostitution exhibiting their body have been reduced to a commodity. This is a trend that has to he checked and fought against. We may not be able to put a stop to this exhibitionism but we must fight and check its growth.

I want to assure all women who are treated inhumanly, who have been denied the human rights and who die in distress that there are sisters and brothers who are concerned for them. I want to tell them that their families and friends are there outside fighting for them and trying to get them back into the mainstream. We know that they have children without their father's name. They are looked down as ''Prostitutes children''. What is their future? Their boys become vagabonds and girls join the same profession. History is repeated and society remains silent.

It is only after an incident that rights are talked about. Processions take place and slogans are shouted. But this is a symptom of a disease that has to be eradicated. If we can rescue the prostitutes and their children then it would be a big service to the humanity. Today we talk about the human rights but we have seen that today human rights is a political weapon and not a cause. I have read a human rights report which indicated that maximum violation of human rights of women have been commmited by the police. The activities of police stations need to be watched very carefully. This can be done by our women's organisations and other voluntary organisations.

Some of us do try to make political capital out of these problems even though we ourselves understand that this should not be so. The society wants that in the direction of solving this problem some stern and serious steps should be taken immediately. I am not a human rights expert, but I call upon all the experts connected with human rights that they should draw out a plan of action. In that plan they should find ways as to how girls and women could be prevented from coming to this profession. There are laws, but how can we prevernt these girls from joining the profession is something that should be looked into. I am saying this because this question is related to the development that is taking place today, to the growth of consumerism. Women's organisations have raised objections against obscene advertisements. This portrayal of women encourages prostitution because it gives justification to these women to continue with the profession.

I am told that in Bombay, bars have been opened which are open till early hours of morning where people dance and sing, and drunk men solicit women by placing money on glases. What is the difference between what was before and now? Earlier also money was kept on the glasses for women to accept in the 'mujara'. So there is no difference between what was happening earlier and now. There is however one difference. Today there is no art form left. Earlier Umrao Jaan and Amrapali commanded respect and were known for their art. History is witness to the fact that their position in society was independent of the respect shown to women in general. They had their own identity. The girls who dance in the night clubs today are just an extension of the advertisement cult, and personification of consumerism its worst form.

I would like the Human Rights Commission and other organisations who are looking into this problem to work out an alternative rehabilitation programme for these women. Small scale industires could be opened for them. I will give full support to these rehabilitation programme if they are put before me. I have the experience of this being earlier in charge of that department. We have had a successful example of this. In South the Devdasis have been rehabilitated and many more are in the process of being rehabilitated.

In order to stop this practice the government enacted a law "Suppression of Immoral Traffic in Women and Girls Act" in 1956. In 1986 a number of amendments were introduced. However, this law without attitudinal changes in the society has had no effect. We talk about this even today. Even today prostitute's children are deprived of education, health and environment. We have to bring in change to ensure that the child is part of the mainstream. Law by itself is no guaranatee of social change. We have to change our mental approach. We have seen that despite the enactment of laws, the changes that it was supposed to have brought about socially and psychologically have not taken place. We are motivating women and have succeeded to some extent. But how we can mobilise them for action and in what manner we will have to deliberate upon and find ways of doing it.

I request all persons and organisations who are concerned with human rights that they should work to stop any act which is against the development of women. The need of the hour which is reflected in the international concern for women and their cause has to be furthered by the young men and women committed to this cause.

With this I thank organisers for inviting me and I want to assure that whenever I am required we can always sit together to further the cause that you have been working for and I must thank you for inviting me.

Ms. Padma Seth, Member, National Commission for Women

I have only a few observations and questions to ask. As a citizen who is participating and an activist who has been interested to alleviate this sort of the problem as I look at the caption "Women in Prostitution: Human Rights Perspectnics", I view it as Women and Human Rights. Wherever they are they have a right to survival, they have a right to dignity and honour and to live a healthy life.

I know that is is common to think that the poor have no future or that their predicament would only get worse. We have to adopt a different approach to prostitution which is a systematic oppression of a particular class of people that is so severe that it can be characterized as structural genocide. But forced prostitution will not continue for ever. That is my forecast and prediction because of the inherent instabilities within the system and the politicisation of prostitution.

The socio-economic colonisation will completely sweep away the exploited. It is a cargo culture. As our Minister has said that in consumerism the human element gets under the carpet. Desperate protectionism is another way of perpetuating this exploiter-exploited syndrome. The development of complexity in human society is an adoptive process. It is also an economic process process. The consequences of social collapse are of course disturbing. The critical factor is whether the society is sustainable with all these ills exploitation. Evolution of strategies that are problem solving and the relationship of the patterns to the evolution of complexity and society is very vital. Today we are addressing ourselves to societal changes and responsibilities. If society has to survive the exploited sections of the society can not be alienated from the people in the region in which they are located. This is a new culture under construction in which we are all participating. There are several factors and actors that are likely to play a role in a continued shaping of the societal values and new structures.

A transdiciplinary and multidimensional approach is necessary. There is no blanket omnibus solution for this. Unless all the systems, specially the police, the administration and the Government put in a determined effort to help these women get rehabilitation either in a home, or a mixed home, or even in our homes, the problem is not going to be solved. The anger and anguish that they carry as outcasts of the society leads them to a retaliatory mood. Even if they are willing to adopt the new ways of living, the prudish society pushes them to the past, thus confining them to a life of damned seclusion and decay.

Packages for rehabilitation by building infrastructures, pumping in resources alone are not going to change the social attitude towards them nor is their low esteem going to evaporate overnight. When there is a vast enemy constantly jeering at their menial job how can you usher in a change in a society characterised by hypocrisy and untruth. Look at the children in the brothels either they are pushed in by their mothers who are in the trade or the children are kidnapped or purchased or brought in as young brides to pursue the flesh trade. How do you rehabilitate them? The Government has formed a core committee all right, but public activists and individuals need to apply their minds to help rehabilitation or else it will be a farcical exercise. How is it that child prostitution has had a tremendous rise and why is it not clamped? How can we rest unless the children are freed from this torture. Why is it that rape of children has become common place today. Police is accountable we say emphatically but the whole society has to help them and give them enough freedom to arrest the customers and the pimps.

In a workshop that was held in collaboration between the National Commission for Women and the National Law School, Bangalore, we suggested that the customers have to be arrested. Many people raised a hue and cry. How many can we arrest? I said arrest them, lock them up inside and let us see. For a week go on arresting them and let that be a deterrent. All the hypocrites who go there in darkness will at least be afraid of even raising their voices.

Rehabilitation package does not mean doling out and putting them in beggar homes or destitute homes and calling them prostitute. Rehabilitation is totally resturcturing minds and psyche for social change. I brought in my own house two girls who had run away from Niketan. I did not people at home who they were. If I had revealed their identity even the educated people at home wouldn't have tolerated.

What I am trying to say is that are we prepared for change. I am not denigrating its importance but what is the rehabilitation package? Are we ready with it? Mr. Amod Kanth rescued those children but what has happened? There was no rehabilitation package. So let us start from the end and come back to the beginning for planning. Planning does not mean just allocating funds and leaving without over seeing its enforcement.

❐ ❐ ❐

2.

TRAFFICKING OF WOMEN AND GIRLS FOR SEXUAL EXPLOITATION AND PREVENTIVE ACTION

The first working session was also chaired by Smt. Mohini Girl. The resource persons were Shri Amond Kanth IPS and Dr. K.K. Mukherjee, Head of the Department of Social Work, university of Delhi.

Smt. Mohini Giri

I will ask Mr. Amond Kanth to speak. He is running an institution called Prayas where he has got 2,880 children. Prayas was stared in 1988 and has 70 non-formal education centres and 16 vocational training centres. They have a health component, a mid day meal component and recreation component. We are indeed very grateful to him for having come here to share his views with us. The topic for the session is 'Trafficking of Women and Girls for Sexual Exploitation and Preventive Action'.

Shri Amond Kanath, IPS

I am again happy to be with the Joint Woment's Programme which is now collaborating with the National Commission for Women.

Before I get on to the subject I will start from the point where Padma Seth left. I have been involved in this kind of activity and problems related to prostitution, particularly children, because as you have been told that I have been engaged in running an organisation which is for neglected children. Many years ago in 1990 there was an event in a red light area of Delhi which became the most memorable event of my life.

This will give you a background on the subject. The Juvenile Justice Act provides that children of certain categories are called neglected children. One of the categories of neglected children are those children who are found in and around the brothel houses, or in a place which is a red light area, or they are in the company of prostitutes and procurers. It is expected of the State and the Government under the Juvenile Justice Act that such disadvantaged children should be picked up from places and taken to the Juvenile Welfare Board. Its is kind of law that exists although as madam Minister said, such laws really do not matter because they are not being implemented. I agree with her.

In this particular case there was a Supreme Court matter pending at that time, Vishal Jeet Vs. Union of India. In this particular public interest litigation, the Supreme Court had demanded of all the State Governments and Police to tell them as to why this particular provision of law was not being implemented. Why the children of prostitutes and those found around red light areas are not being picked by the State or not being sent to the Juvenile Welfare Board. One of the queries was addresed to the Commissioner of Police, Delhi and as I was Deputy Commissioner of Police (Crime), it came down to me. The petitioiner in that public litigation petition, Vishaljeet an advocate, came to me and insisted that I should take action regarding these children.

I consulted Sarla Mudgal and also the chairmam of the Juvenile Welfare Board, Dr. B.L. Kantroo. I told them that the provision of law states that such children should be rescued and taken away from such kinds of areas and produced; before the Juvenile Welfare Board. He said "All right, bring them"

First of all I conducted a survey in that area. For the outsiders let me inform you that Delhi has the biggest red light area in this country. it is located at the GB Road starting from the place called Farash Khana down to the place called Ajmeri Gate. There are 22 flats or kothas as they are called, where prostitutes live with their children and families. With the help of some social workers, who worked in that area at that time, we conducted surveys and found that there were some minor girl children who were living there and were gradually being being inducted into protitution. We organised a group in which we had 40 lady police officers, one lawyer, and half a dozen social workers. We then went to the place and conducted a raid in early morning. In that exercise there were 111 children who were picked up from the red light area and brought to the police head quarters.

This led to a major crisis because there are about 10 to 15,000 people who are dependent directly on this trade in this red light area. When these children were brought to the police station there was a demonstration at the police station. The entire media was after it and these women claimed that these children belonged to them. The lady police officers and others talked to the children in person and it was found that of 111 children at least 91 were such who did not belong to women living in that area. Obviously they were brought there or were kidnapped and were in the process of becomming prostitutes.

We produced these children before the Juvenile Welfare Board. I requested the local LNJP Hospital to create a board before which these children could be produced for medical examination to find out whether they were children or not. As you know below the age of 16 somebody is called a child, 16 to 18 he is minor, beyond 18 he becomes a major. The Immoral Traffic Prevention Act applies to all of them.

Finally we produced these children before the Juvenile Welfare Board. There was a demonstration in the red light area that created a problem for Dr. Kantroo and his group.

Their medical examination could not be done properly. The only exercise that we could do was a kind of personal inteview conducted by the lady officers jointly with the social workers and found that 91 of them were actually children of these 91 out of 111 were those who did not have their parents living in the red light area. No medical examination could be conducted. Dr. Kantroo and his team failed to control the situation. therefore they were sent to the observation home. The observation home had such a big crowd and could not cope with his kind of load and they were let off within 3 or 4 days. It was an exercise that was probably being done for the fist time in the country. The law does not allow even the mothers to keep their children. If you even grant a concession to the mothers that their children can be kept there even then 91 out of 111 were definitely not children whose mothers were from that area.

This event has cast a deep shadow on my mind and it has been there ever since. The whole system and framework of law, the framework of rehabilitation, the framework of juvenile rehabilitation is inadequate today. In the last 10 years that I know about this area, I have observed there are very few organisations and individuals working in the area. I am happy Jyotsna ji that so many people today have come who are associated with this problem. there is only one school that is running now in the red light area and that is by Lalita of JWP.

When you talk about trafficking of women I can give you figures also. In 1988 we had 15,989 cases which involved 2700 men and 15430 women. Under the Immoral Traffic Prevention Act the total number of women were 75% of those arrested,in comparison to men who were 25% of the total. In 1989 there were 13466 cases and only 4462 men and 13900 women were arrested. The total number arrested were 18162. The woman or the so called prostitute is a victim of the entire situation. In majority of cases, she becomes the accused. I do not know to sort this issue even as a policeman. If this entire enactment

Immoral Traffic Prevetion Act is meant to safeguard her interest and save her from being sexually exploited than how is it answering the needs? I think the fault lies partly with the police also because they are not able to investgate or register as many cases against men as against women.

There are many seasons. Majority of these cases are actually being registered under section 8 of the Immoral Traffic Prevention Act, that is soliciting. That is easy. If a woman is seen soliciting in a red light area on the roadside then she can be arrested on the grounds of soliciting. For the customers and the prime movers of the system, punishment is only 7 days in all under the Act. The creator of the demand for prostitution is hardly ever punished. The 1992 figures indicate that 12595 cases that were registered. In the first case the number of cases that are being registered are not high even though its is the national figure. Second that arrests that are being made are of women.

While talking about this whole question of the trade of prostitution we also include the call girl racket. It is a highly organised activity. Its ramifications are within the district or the city, within the state and inter-state. Majority of women and girls who come to the red light area are either kidnapped or enticed. Even if the person enticed or is a minor, it amounts to kidnapping. 70 to 75% of the people who come to these areas are kidnapped and brought there.

Another sad part the problem is that 75% kidnapped people are women. Only 25% are boys. In fact this whole trade of prostitution and its racket is very pervasive. When we talk about the women and pimps arrested or taken to courts and let off on bail, the same women and men come back to the trade and there is a vicious circle which goes on a nationwide scale. Majority of these girls who are found at one place for e.g. in Bombay , you can't detect them in Bombay once they are caught because the addresses given are wrong, fingerprints are not there, and the women ultimately move to Calcutta,

Madras and back to Bombay after some time. The whole trade goes on like this. There is no permanent solution even from the enforcement point of view.

The second kind of women are the Bangla Deshis and Nepalese. All of you who have worked in the red light areas know that the number of Nepali girls in this area is very large. Certain areas in the country produce majority of prostitutes like Tamil Nadu, Karnataka, Andhra Pradesh, Kerala and Bihar. This is according to the figures available. From these areas majority of such women come and they spread all over the country. They are spread all over the country.

The brothel house is a place for prostitution which is used for sexual abuse and exploitation of the prostitute. Earlier the definition of prostitution was different. Now the definition of the profession is that any kind of commercial activity with respect to women for sexual exploitation and abuse or for commercial gains is considered to be prostitution. A woman can be an object of exploitation and abuse under the new act, whereas in the previous act the definition was very simple that any woman who offers her body for sexual intercourse she was considered a prostitute. The amended law clarifiers the point on exploitation of the woman.

The law in no more about suppression, it is about prevention - the Immoral Traffic Prevention Act. So when we are talking about the subject it is clear that the present law talks about the prevention of the entire malady. This law again distinguishes the child, minor and major. Punishments are stringent. Since this problem is inter-state in nature we have a trafficking police officer. This new position has been created who has the jurisdiction all over the country. The courts and the police also can now investigate into cases which earlier could not be investigated. This problem of inter-state ramification has been understood now.

With regard to the punishments let me inform you that

they are stringent. If somebody is found responsible for child prostitution the punishment is life sentence. Seven years is mandatory. In respect of majors also if it is found that a woman was enticed or brought into prostitution or forced into prostitution the punishment could be upto 14 years. This act could be read with the Juvenile Justice Act and with reference to the exercise we undertook in 1990, that if any child or any minor is found in the red light area the presumption would be that with respect to this child an offence has been created under the Immoral Prevention Act. No child can be kept can be kept in a brothel in the red light area. After a medical examination if it is found that the child was sexually abused again the presumption would be that in respect of that child or minor there was sexual exploitation. Another change that has been made is that power has been given to the licensing authority to suspend or cancel the licence of a hotel which has been used as brothel. When we come to the recommendations it is often asked why hotels only. Ms. Sahi said that there are many places where such activities are going on and probably cancellation could be of other places also.

When we talk about the police point of view it is better to know the problems the police face. Basically the police say that they lack public support. They themselves are also responsible for that. The NGOs and the voluntary organisations and those who are in the trade itself, the brothel keepers and others tirelessly blame the police for denial of justice. The police also feel that the public and these people who have vested interest are damaging their cause but not permitting the police to act. Again the police says that there is excessive interference of various organisations, delayed justice, and undue publicity. These are the various areas in which police is finding it difficult and they feel that they are not able to exercise powers under the Immoral Traffic Prevention Act because they do not have the right kind of support. When they really talk of the entire problem, as I told you earlier, the police and others also feel that unless we create some kind of rehabilitation structure it is not possible to take the law to its logical conclusion. Ms. Sahi also talked about some kind of gainful employment. As of now in the whole country except in few areas where certain rehabilitation packages have been created, there is hardly any provision for rehabilition of these women. Most rehabilitation programmes are extremely short-sighted. When I talked to them not as a police officer but as an ordinary person very few came forward to say that they wanted to go away from there. There must be reasons why these women are not prepared to go from there. This indicated that you have to create conditions which are more attractive and fulfilling, which have some hope for the future. This is why when the police acts one major problem that they face is when they record the statements of these women or the young children as to whether they gave been kept there forcibly or how they come there. Invariably in 9 out of 10 cases they say they are there of their own accord. When we go there as individual social workers and talk to them at length, they might tell you their sad life story, but that comes later. It is not possible for the police and enforcement agencies to bring out that kind of story in a recorded statement. It is clear that these women are not wanted anywhere else. They cannot go back to their homes, their own parents or families because they are not wanted there. We have to create conditions where they can be rehabilitated.

Before I conclude I would like to share some recommendations which I found very useful. These are:

— Punishment to the customers is inadequate.

— Evidence of senior police officers should be admitted. As of now any statement made to a police officer is not admitted.

— Delayed trial is a major reason why problems are created and therefore these may be tried on a summary basis.

— There should not be any adjournments as such.

— About the cancellation of the licences, police should have the authority to cancel the licences of the night clubs, hotel parlours, etc. which are being used for this purpose.

— Incidents should be carefully probed to find out where the police has gone wrong and what all has happened.

— An Advisory Committee be formed as suggested in the Immoral Traffic Prevntion Act with police officers and the social workers. This committee so far is non existent. In Delhi also it is not there. This kind of Advisory Committee must be formed.

— To identify pimps and procurers who run the trade, and to keep them on record somewhere. There should be some kind of a national data bank where the photographs and fingerprints of such people could be kept.

— Shelter homes should be set up in each district. Minimum standards for these shelter homes be fixed. The conditions today are appalling. The management should include intervention of voluntary organisations who can participate in these activities.

— The training of these women in other vocations be made on more concrete lines so that gainful employment is created for them.

— Some kind of follow up action be taken for those discharged from these shelter homes.

— About the children of the prostitutes it has been categorically said that they be provided education, hostels be provided.

What is more important is that the police, the juvenile boards, the judiciary has to be sensitised about this issue and children should be removed.

— Public interest has to be aroused in this matter.

About acquittals two point were raised. Generally the courts expect very extreme degrees of proof whereas the law does nort require it. Law provides for presumptions. The courts are expecting the same level of proofs which is applied in other cases. The presumption, of course, should be definitely implemented. When we talk of ordinary criminals, the burden of proof is for the prosecution to establish. In the ITPA there is presumption to some extent, the burden of proof passes on to persons like the brothel people. But in actual practice the law is not very clear. Probably if this kind of proof shifts on them, then the situation that obtains today, that 76% of those accused and arrested are women, would not be there. In the correct perspective the number of men arrested should be 70 to 90% and women should be less.

In conclusion I would only say that we cannot continue to have the situation like the one that obtains today. I am against any kind of legalisation of this trade because you just can't bargain on somebody's conscience or instincts. You just can't legalise the act of women offering her body to be used or abused or exploited sexually. The idea beyond my comprehension.

Dr. K.K. Mukherjee

I represent Gram Niyojan Kendra, a voluntary action organisation working at Ghaziabad. I am also professor and Head of the Department of Social work, delhi University. I have the dubious distinction of conducting two statewise studies on prostitution, of Uttar Pradesh and of Delhi. My experience shows that there is hardly any action for the prostitutes, particularly aiming at prevention of the problem. this comes after they are trapped. Do you want them to be trapped and then talk abount it?

Many of us feel that there are definitely women who are more vulnerable to the threat. We know definite areas in the country, definite number of villages. This is clear from my studies. The Central Social Welfare Board conducted the studies in the metropolitan cities of India. I was asked to compile an all-India perspective.

Before I talk about prevention I would like to make some observations. Do you know the number of girls and women entering into this trade everyday? The number is an approximation because nobody has done an all-India study, but nearly 200 girls and women everyday enter this trade. Ever year about 75,000 women enter this trade and two third of them that is 80% come because of situational compulsions. It is not because they wanted to enter but because they are forced into it. Sometimes there are socio-psychological reasons, sometimes it is because of the network of this trade which forced them to join. If we consider this situation, prevention is a must and it is possible.

The moment we talk about trafficking it is a violation of law. Trafficking involves sale and purchase of women for sexual purposes. If we stop trafficking by initiating a number of provisions it can be prevented. Prevention need not be a myth but a reality. The question is what do you want to prevent? What are the facilities available for prevention?

Yesterday's prostitution and today's prostitution are not the some phenomena. Today 20 to 34% women enter the trade on their own because of the change in the value system, privatisation, consumerism, and change in the whole attitude towards sex. But 80% of them are compelled. In Delhi between 1954 to 1992 the population has increased 4 times, and the population of prositutes has increased 17 times. If we see the trends in all the cities we can see that there is tremendous increase of women this trade in all these years. This lends credence to my appeal to you that recognise that this as preventable and there must be urgency in preventing that. I am not saying that it can be abolished totally but it is preventable.

The red light area system of functioning is changing. New cities and towns do not have red light areas. When we talk about strategies don't think in terms of the present day system because what you work out today would be workable after five years. The new city authorities would refuse that they have red light areas. People working today in the red light areas feel that it is not a profitable economic proposition. If they work as call girls it is much more profitable. There is a great freedom of operation and there is more income. Call girls also are not illiterate girls. Yesterday's scenario where illiteracy and poverty psychologically encouraged prostitution has changed today. Tomorrow the prostitutes will not operate from the red light area. All areas of the city could be vulnerable points. Any neighbour of ours may be in the trade because we do not know as we live in the culture of anonymity. The problems of the children, the stigmatisation etc., will change also along with the change in the function of prostitutes. In Delhi we all know, the prostitutes in the red light areas do not keep their children. All prostitues do no have children. Those who have children do not want their children to enter postitution. It is situational compulsion. They do not consider the girl child as economic investment. They make their maximum effort to keep their children away from the profession in a number of ways. Sometimes they send their children to the hostels, somtimes to the parents home, sometimes they keep them in separate houses in Delhi. So we have to understand this mechanism if we are dealing with the children of the prostitutes. Getting the children of the prostitutes from the red light areas is yesterday's proposition not today's.

We all know that the prostitution phenomena is multidimensional. People list 19 to 20 factors. Prostitution is not caused by a single factor it is an interplay of number of factors. These factors keep on changing. It is because of sociocultural economic factors. It is cultural because there are a number of castes in India who voluntarily accept prostitution and they do not condemn their girls from entering into the trade.

If these are the reasons and causes our preventive strategies have to be multidimensional. We cannot think of a single dimensional approach. In India, out of 378 districts one-third are drought prone areas and produce about the two-third of the girls and women who come into prostitution and work in the metropolitan cities.

We know the places from where they come. We have submitted the list of villages to the Government of india. Can we think of doing something at that level? Red light areas would be redundant in a period of time. Ultimately when we think of the prevention of the problem we have to plug the new system.

What would be the answer to this problem? We have to go back to the rural development programme. Government for the past so many years has been talking about the area development programme. We know from which places they come and why they are coming. Why don't we provide those facilities at that place so that they do not come.This area development approach is the most important strategy in terms of prevention.

Since alternatives are limited, once you enter the profession getting out of it and getting social recognition is not easy. However, there are courageous women and girls who want to come out of that. We have to evolve proper rehabilitation programmes. In terms of this prostitution problem there are certain aspects, certain activities, which are very glamorous. Many organisations go for things like arranging marriages which invariably fail without follow-up action. These are soft options in terms of rehabilitation. Ultimately when we have to think in terms of rehabilitation of these girls we have to have a package programme. This package would include education, health, vocational training, employment opportunities, legal aid, etc. There has to be a package which should be provided in rotation.

Trafficking is a law order problem. Our study says that District Magistrates, Senior Superintendents of Police, do not give importance to this phenomena of prostitution. We have moved from suppression to prevention. There is change. Amod Kanth would know that only 10% of the District Magistrates may have read the new Act. Who will then implement it? Judiciary is not interested. Police is interested because it gives money. The whole system of trafficking has linkage from the village to the top level.

Jyotsana ji told me that on the days of dharmas this business booms in the red light areas. Delhi being capital all parties want to have rallies. Delhi is also a big business centre. Once they come they bring other women from thier own areas because of the demand. We have to stop that if anybody has to take the blame it is we educated people. We are good at talking but we do not do the minimum thing. Today in villages touts move to arrange marriage of daughters. People who do not have money to spend, fall prey to this. In the name of some money the father is lured and daughter is brought to Delhi. In the name of jobs girls are brought to Delhi. We all know about it but can't we do something?

We can do a few things that will go a long way. Don't consider prevention to be the responsibility of the police, Government and non-govt agencies. Basically it is the responsibility if the people themselves. We get intellectual pleasure in discussing the issue and not doing anything. Accept the fault that we have allowed it to continue.

Can we not think in term of educating people at our own level? Traffickers operate vulnerable places like the railway station, lonely women and single women. They try to get friendly with single women. Can we educate the girls? Any woman is vulnerable. They say do not take laddoo at the railway station otherwise you may lose your luggage. You must tell them that they would be led into a problem if they get lured by strangers. Can we have a citizen's committee? The committee can check these people moving at the railway stations and other areas and keep a watchful eye on them. These are certain things that people can also do.

This is not the job of the Government alone. Government will only make promises because the official machinery will be more interested in making money and not doing any justice to them. There will always be good officers but their number is less. These studies were conducted at the instance of Central Social Welfare Board. I moved from pillar to post and we asked for programme support. They said that they do not have funds to support. Prostitution can bring in easy money but it is better to have the other modes of life and go for alternate vocations. That will take time. it will take ten to fifteen years to change attitudes in order to make a change in this direction.

Despite Government apathy we have started communication with our linkage groups. We know certain areas in Nepal and Sonali near Gorakhpur where exchange takes place every day. The police is part of the game and they help girls and women to cross over. We know organisations bordering Nepal and Gorakhpur and bounderies of Bengal. We are trying to develop linkages with these places. Nepali girls are in demand here because age does not get reflected in their facial appearance. Prostitution is a phenomena of age. 80% of the prostitutes are below 18 years because anybody who invests in them wants returns and a middle aged woman cannot get you the return. Emphasis is to get a girl prostitute of younger age in the network.

The Government said that we take dairy development programmes and poultry farming. Can a total integrated programme which would call for an attitudinal change and programmes requires change.

DISCUSSION

Pramila Dandavate, Ex M.P., Samajwadi Mahila Sobha,

You cannot solve the problem of the sick society by giving medicine alone, what is required is prevention. It is important that we realise how genuine we are in finding a solution to this malaise. Are we doing it just for the sake of image building ?

I would like to open this discussion instead and request you to raise the issues. We have with us police officer who has tries to do something through his own agency and the other is a scholar who after doing research is trying to take action.

Khairati Lal Bhola, New Delhi,

The Government of India has introduced Panchayati Raj in 1993 and has given 30 % representation to women. To stop trafficking I think women at the village level should look into this matter and maintain statistics of these women who are entering this trade. The Government should initiate measures by asking women at the Panchayat level to look into matter seriously.

Padma Seth

Mr. Kanth, you have spoken about how you retrieved the children who were taken to the LNJP Hospital where medical examination was not possible. why was it not possible?

Amod Kanth

The LNJP Hospital did make arrangements for the medical examination. they asked the Juvenile Welfare Board to present a fixed number of children. But the Board buckled under the pressure of the prostitutes, pimps and procurers and they released all children within two days. So there was no opportunity to send them to the hospital.

Padma Seth

Why I raised this question is because everyone is talking about the police and carelessness of everybody including ourselves but we are not pinpointing the medical jurists. They are the real culprits in the game. They remove the whole evidence. I am emphasising this point because the danger starts.

The second question is to Dr. Mukherjee. You said that we must have citizens' committees for prevention. For this long range planning is also important. I would like to share with you that the National Commission for Women fomulated a bill called Marriage Bill which applies to all religions, in which compulsory registration was incorporated. In this no girl under the age 18 can register, also, registration is compulsory within 3 days or else severe punishment has been stipulated.

Dr. K.K. Mukherjee

This a law that would always remain on paper. What are the infrastructural facilities in the remote villages? They have not seen the Block Development Officer for years.

Padma Seth

But when you can register birth and deaths why not marriage?

K.K. Mukherjee

Birth registration helps in ration card facility and education of the children. Marriage does not have any advantage of registration.

Arun Bhandari, AIDS Bhed-Bhav Virodhi Andolan,

Five years back in the red light area Mr. Amod Kanth violated the JJ Act and took away 112 women in which there were 70 girls, For the last five tears a struggle for them has been going on. We have come to this meeting armed with all the material pertaining to this case and would like to distribute the same at this meeting. Whatever Mr. Kanth has said in this meeting may have some meaning and we do feel that there is a definite change in your approach. But would you like to come out openly in public and admit that what you did then was wrong and we shall withdraw the case against you.

Amod Kanth

This entire exercise started with the orders of the Supreme Court of India, the highest court of the land. For your information this entire operation of mine was put before the Supreme Court of India and the Court has put on record an appreciation of the work done by me. It is on record and it is not for you to decide on it. When the Supreme Court of the India has appreciated the work done by me I don't think any lower court can pass any judgement against me.

Secondly there is no question of asking for forgiveness because I did something right and in accordance with law.

Elizabeth Vatsyan, AIDS Awareness Group

I know a lot of neglected children who are not in GB Road, they are not in the brothels. I see them in our locality where seemingly respectable people like us have no time for our children. How do you say the neglected children are only in the brothels?

Amod Kanth

That was not my point. There were five categories of neglected children. The children in the red light area are only one of the categories. Since they are living in a difficult situation, they should be given prority.

Shobha Sakharwade, PRAKRITI

Dr. Mukherjee there are many organisations which are working in the area but are unaware of the ground realities. This is true of orgnisations which are functioning outside bigger cities. How can we create an atmosphere through awareness outside these big cities?

Dr. K.K. Mukherjee

It is good that you have raised this question. Prostitution even as a study is a neglected field. It is stigmatised and people conducting these studies are not appreciated as intellectuals.

I will tell you my experience of Delhi and UP. When I was doing this study I was helped in my Delhi study by Jyotsna ji. However a number of leading women activists whom I approached asked why I was doing this? Is it an issue, they asked.

Pramila Dandavate

I want to say one thing that if we do not consider the effect of globalisation and new economic order our efforts at preventive measures will not carry any weight. We must assess the effect of the easy money and consumerism that is on the increase in society. Perhaps in future more women will be voluntary prostitutes than forced prostitutes. This is bound to happen.

You must think of the strategy for the future. I do not want to go into details at this stage but I would like you to consider this predicament. I thank the main speakers who have really opened a Pandora's Box of questions. I am sure answeres will be there. I would only say that the law by itself will never bring the change in the society. We have fought against the dowry menace and yet dowry deaths are on the increase. Let us not totally depend on law. Law helps only to check and not prevent.

3.
THE LAWS REGARDING PROSTITUTION : NATIONAL AND INTERNATIONAL

This session was chaired by Prof. Lotika Sarkar of the Centre for Women's Development Studies. The resource persons for the session were Jean D'Cunha, noted sociologist, Ms. Ratna Kapur, a lawyer and Dr. Ved Kumari of Delhi University.

Prof. Lotika Sarkar

The subject of the session is "The Laws Regarding Prostitution". There is a great debate that has been going on for sometime as to whether prostitution should be made illegal or whether there should be criminalisation of it.

There have been three approaches to the entire question-on, criminalise it, in other words have more criminal sanctions to stop prostitution all together. The second is legalisation whereby you have to register and get a licence. The third one is one which is favoured by most and that is decriminalisation. This means repeal all laws that deal with prostitution because prostitution is not a crime or an activity that requires a licence. Let us decriminalise it all together and try and understand as to why there is prostitution.,

Poverty leads to prostitution. Secondly, in this male dominated society it will be difficult to do away with postitution, because as the Law Commission said while making its report that we must continue to have prostitution otherwise it will be a great danger to family life. Now men can go to the prostitutes, but if you criminalise it then they will break up other families. If you believe in the family you should contine with prostitution.

Jean D'Cunha, University of Bombay

My task here is to present first an overview of the present laws governing prostitution, namely the Immoral Traffic Prevention Act of 1986 and secondly my reflections on the whole question of legalising prostitution. In the morning session Mr. Kanth has exposed the law and so I do not want to dwell on that. I would start talking about the second point of my presentation.

A dominant perspective in this whole discourse and that is a position that I critique is a view that asserts that prostitution is an expression of a woman's autonomy and self determination. This view maintains that:

1) The division between the wives and women in prostitution is an artifical construction because all women in a patriarchal society are sexually objectified.
2) It asserts that in a patriarchal, structured and defined job market which is characterised by male preference in jobs, low paid jobs and repetitive mechancial jobs for women at the lower end of the hierarchy, a woman's entry into prostitution is a free, conscious, deliberate, entrepreneurial choice.
3) This view asserts that in such a job market which is defined by patriarchy women are oriented or recruited into women-oriented jobs that reinforce trait and role sterotypes of women. so why then are we singling out women in prostitution as pandering to male ego or male domination?

Against this background this view argues for removal of all forms of discrimination and stigmatisation of women in prostitution both formal and informal. Secondly, this view asserts that they wish to protect the rights of women in prostitution. They then go further to argue that the right of women to prostitution is a fundamental human right and prostitution must be a legitimate, valid, acceptable form of labour. This is an expression of a woman's human right.

Further they argue, that the whole institution of prostitution including third party management must be decriminalised. It should be brought outside the purview of criminal law and subject to labour law like all other business.

Lastly, they assert that separate trafficking laws must be introduced to penalise traffickers and this must be distinct and separate from general laws governing free choice prostitution.

I alongwith with several other groups have problems with this position.

1. This position is framed within the contours of a liberal feminist theory that takes sexual discrimination or gender discrimination as given. It doesn't draw links between and economic bases of prostitution and wider social, economic and political process. As we all know that the ground level points to far greater complexities in terms of degrees of freedom, degrees of choice and degrees of coercion on a continuum rather than on neat categories of free prostitution and forced prostitution. Further we need to demystify structural conditions that compel a woman into prostitution and keep her in prostitution to arive at what is really meant by the so called free choice.

2. This free-forced dichotomy is largely a western construction which seeks to normalise prostitution in society really ignoring the reality of our halves of the globe where large masses of women are lugged into the poverty-trafficking nexus because of ignorance and poverty. This situation is going to become more acute in the context of globalisation and our structural adjustment policies.

3. This view collapses the distinction between the individual in prostitution and the institution of prostitution. It wants to decriminalise not just the individual but the entire institution. This legitimises the exploitative, the patriarchal basis of prostitution.

Regardless of the fact that a woman enters the prostitution freely or not, the very condition of sexual objectification or sexual commodification of woman's body and sex is depersonalisation and dehumanisation, a condition of alienation of violation one's physical bodily and mental integrity and dignity. Also women in prostitution who enter prostitution 'freely' are not free from client violence and state violence. This is a violation of her human right. In sanctioning the institution we are legitimising third party management which is the real exploiter of the sex service sector. In parts of South Asia where the brothel is a dominant form of prostitution characterised by conditions of confinement and bondage we will be legitimising exploitation of women in prostitution.

There is a distinction made between free prostitution and legitimising it and trafficking laws to penalise traffickers and forced prostitution. What is missed is the close connection between trafficking and the sex service etablishment because trafficking is a principled means of supply of the sexual labour of women and children into the sex service sector. If you are going to legalise prostitution you are going to have a spurt in trafficking. There is a positive correlation between the two and this has been documented throughout the 19th century when prostitution was legalised in Europe. Also there are serious problems in applying these trafficking laws because one cannot say where force begins and freedom ends. A girl/woman after having been trafficked into prostitution exist in conditions of confinement and bondage, and may attain a certain degree of social mobility within prostitution and get higher in the hierarchy. How do you apply these laws and where do you apply them?

The experience of all countries that have legalised prostitution has shown that women have not benefited from this system. This demand has been largely articulated by the controllers and promoters of sex service sector.

My own point of view and the point of view of several other groups in India and internationally is to keep our existing law, the Immoral Traffic Prevention Act with modifications. The modifications are:

1. Delete penal sanctions against individual women in prostitution.

2. Penal sanctions against the racketeers must be there. IPTA raises penal measures against racketeers but it makes little sense to raise penal measures if we do not really give teeth to our implementing structurres. All of us know that the police are the implementing apparatus and vested with a large amount of power with respect to implementation of our current laws. We have no illusions about the quality of implementaticn. We suggest the establishment of statutory and mandatorily constituted citizens' committees which work with the police. This may lead to some kind of efficacy in implementation.

3. Magistrates under the present law have discretionary powers to lower sentences below the minimum. These discretionary powers must be eliminated if implementation has to be effective.

4. We must have gender sensitisation programmes at every level of implementation for all implementing authorities.

5. The current orientation towards rehabilitation in our present law stresses on reformation and correction. We ought to change this perspective with respect to rehabilitation in order to look at the women, children and individuals in prostitution as human beings who are victims and survivors of exploitative situation. Particularly individuals who have

been trafficked are in conditions of confinement and bongage. We need to provide infra structural facilities to facilitate emotional, physical and economic reintegration.

6. If our present law which stresses prevention has to be really taken seriously then we have to address ourselves to prevention in terms of addressing economic and social policies and cultural attitudes and values which can safegurad the economic rights of women, critique consumerist attitudes and sexist values in society. Internationally there are several groups in India and abroad spearheaded by the Coalition against Trafficking in Women. They have put forth new convention on prostitution which is a total rehauling of the 1949 convention before the UN for consideration. This convention looks at prostitution as a form of violence against women, it argues for dropping all penal measures against women or individuals in prostitution, penalising racketeers, tightening up the implementation structures, and seriously addrressing the question of prevention and rehabitation.

Ratna Kapur

I will first give you an overview of what is there internationally. There is the International Convention for the Suppression of Trafficking in Women and Children, 1921 and 1933, amended by UN in 1947. The Convention that exists and has been ratified by Government of India is about the Suppression of Traffick in Persons and of the Exploitatin of Others, 1950. The objectives that were stated in the preamble are:

1. Securing dignity and worth of the human person,
2. The welfare of individual, family and community.

So you have both the indivudual concern as well as the moral concern which is enshrined in this Convention. I am glad that there is a new overhaul of this Convention because at the time the Convention was adopted and ratified there of no thinking of prostitutes as sex workers. It is only in the past 20 years that sex workers have participated in debates which concern their rights and lives. Unfortunately most of the Conventions that we hold are without these women.

The next set of rights that came into being internationally had to do with right of women against violence. This is a declaration which was passed by the UN General Assembly in December 1993 after the UN Conference on Human Rights.

The final document was the Convention on the Elimination of All Forms of Discrimination against Women which came into force in 1981 was ratified by the Government of India only in 1993.

These documents are very important because they have involved women who have been subjected to discrimination of violence. Therefore in my opinion, they should be given more importance and should influence policy decision and formulation of law.

Let me just describe some of these liberal positions which Jean has touched upon:

There is a radical view which considers prostitution as some form of female sexual slavery and as a form of violence against women. They see a woman in prostitution as a victim. Their terminology is related to that kind of response. They also urge that this system of prostitution is supported by pimps, brothel keepers and the Mafia. This is why it asks for stricter regulations and increased penalities against the mafia, pimps and brothel keepers. Although the concern here is with women it is also unfortunate that this view coincides with what the moral right wing is saying. Its concern is not with women but with the threat or the danger to the family.

The second perspective is socialist oriented. It is concerned with the fact that prostitution is a result of women's economic impoverishment. Women therefore are forced into this kind of work .

The liberal view is based on the rights perspective which states that we do away with the laws that exist and allow women to be subjected to same laws as any other workers. These are the positions that are taken by the sex workers and feminists in the West and in East.

It is interesting to note how these approaches get reflected in law and I can briefly state what those approaches are:

1. First is the criminalisation approach which we are all familiar and uncomfortable with. This criminalisation approach is also divided into two categories of either abolition or toleration. Abolition has some moral basis. The prostituties are contemptible and we should do everything to abolish their very existence. Toleration is different and it is not concerned whether the activity is legal or illegal but is more concerned with criminalising outward manifestations of prostitution or sex work like soliciting and trafficking that is the subject matter at the end of this law. Because women will not testify against those who are their clients or their keepers if they have no alternative and the state is not giving them any rights protection. They are prosecuted in the process. That is the flaws within the law and Jean has also addressed certain aspects that need modification.

2. The legalisation approach has been misunderstood to a great extent. It is based on the assumption that there needs to be a balance drawn between public health and public need. The paramaters within which legalisation is based, i.e. licensing, mandatory check-ups, all violate women's human rights. Legalisation has been misunderstood to the extent that it only gives more power to the state in legalising these women to fulfil a public need.

3. We are very much in favour of the decriminalisation approach. It is based on the assumption that prostitution is

a personal choice and it is a personal matter between the consenting adults. There was a significant international meeting of the sex workers who wanted this approach and they want all penalising laws abolished and be subjected to workers protection legislations. The advantage of this approach is that it makes a distinction between the individual in prostitution and the institution of prostitution. I think that in the other approaches of criminalisation and legalisation this distinction is observed.

If you see the international documents the most important document is the Convention on the Elimination of All Kinds of Discrimination Against Women. That document spells out equality in a way that is not restricted to giving women formal rights but dealing with substantive notions of equality. It emphasises that women as a group and some sections of the women have been historically disadvantaged by virtue of their gender. Therefore the state needs to adopt certain temporary special measures which will help to eliminate that discrimination.

In the case of women in prostitution they have been discriminated against by virtue of their gender and also by the nature of their work. Therefore the equality doctrine that is enshrined states that we must give certain rights and measures for the women who are already there in prostitution. We need to produce some affirmative action policy which would include their right to liberty, not to be kept in isolation or quarantine, not to be forcibly medically examined, right not to be denied health facilities, the right to retain custody of their children. In this talk about women in sex work threatening the families we often forget that women in sex work have families too. It is just that she does not get the benefit and she only gets the burdens of the family system.

The moment you start treating women as victims, they are excluded from all processes and you invite the whole apparatus of criminal law to come and address that kind of violence. Violence is addressed by the criminal law not the civil law. We need to talk about it in terms of discrimination. This is a more healthy way and it sets up link with all women who are discriminated against by vitue of their gender and perhaps by their caste or class ethnicity. I see no problem in giving women rights in order to fight the exploitation and violence that takes place. If you do not give them rights in the first place how will they fight?

Prof. Lotika Sarkar

You have heard the two sides of the problem. One was Jean in which she said that Immoral Traffic Prevention Act be strengthened, deleting the provisions that are against women, and now the international side also. Now I ask Ved Kumari to speak.

Dr. Ved Kumari, Faculty of Law, Delhi University

I shall be dealing with the provisions which exist in the Constitution and the ITPA.

1. Article 21 of the Constitution gives the right to life with dignity.
2. Article 23 of the Constitution grants the fundamental right against exploitation, and trafficking in human beings has been prohibited.
3. By article 35 the Parliament has been empowered to pass legislation against any action which violates any fundamental right. This right has not been given to the state Government. The provision of ITPA comes under that.
4. By article 39 of the Constitution it is the fundamental duty of all to renounce practices which are derogatoy to the dignity of women and that humanism and compassion be practised.

The Suppression of Immoral Traffic Act, 1956 which was introduced after 1951 Convention, was amended in 1986 to become Immoral Traffic Prevention Act, Jean said that it is difficult to make a distinction between voluntary and forced prostitution. If you notice, free choice prostitution means the sexual exploitation or abuse of a person for commercial purposes. Legislation talks about two categories of persons, one who are considered as victims and the others who are offenders. The victims include the rescued or detained women who are forcibly kept in the brothels. For offenders, many offences have been listed like running brothels, allowing use of premises, living on the earning of the prostitutes, procuring for the purpose of prostitution, detaining in brothels, prostitution in public place, seducing and soliciting in the public place, seduction in custody, non-compliance of eviction of brothels, running correctional institutions without licence and contravening any of the rules under this legislation. The amended law provides for minimum punishment of 7 years and even up to life. In many provisions discretion has been allowed for special reasons in which punishment could be less than 7 years. Our biases do creep in because of this discretion.

Under Section 8 of the ITPA, the punishment for seducing and soliciting for the purposes of prostitution for the first time is six months imprisonment or fine upto Rs.500, on second conviction punishment till one year and fine up to Rs.500. However if the same offence is committed by a man, he is punished for a period not less than 7 days. It is 7 days for man and 6 months for a woman. For a man it may extend to 3 months and for a woman it is one year. While we claim to be gender neutral I fail to understand why this discrepancy is there.

To check trafficking changes were effected in the I.P.C. The very fact that offences have been incorporated in the I.P.C. shows that this problem has been taken a serious turn. It has been taken seriously only to the point where there is a sale of a minor girl, by importing from abroad or procurement from within the country for the purposes of illicit intercourse or prostitution.

Coming to the provisions regarding the enforcement machinery under I.T.P.A., Special Police Officers can be appointed not below the rank of Inspector by the Central and State Governments to check trafficking. A new category of Trafficking Officers has now ben introduced who have been specifically authorised for having been given the responsibility of checking inter-state trafficking. This effectivencess is only for the NGOs working in the field to assess. This provision lays down that NGOs should be involved in search operations which may be conducted without warrant in the presence of two respectable neighbours.

It is also provided that only women police officers may interrogate women and children. If a woman policeofficer is not available a male officer can do so only in the presence of a lady member of a recognised welfare institution. The law provides for intermediate custody in corrective homes or with NGOs. The intention of calling a neighbour or to associate an NGO is to ensure that there is no harassment of these women while a search is being conducted. But if you notice most of the offences are not only for checking trafficking but those which check the profession itself. The law does not impose a ban on the trade but makes it clear that it would not facilitate the trade and instead obstruct the trade. This implies that if you want the trade to go on you bribe the police. A ban is not envisaged because it would be against the interest of men and their family. I would like to question the approach which believes that families are saved because men can go to these women to satisfy their lust if they are disatisfied with women at home.

I would like to refer to the raid made by Amod Kanth. The raid was carried out at the instance of the writ petition by Vishaljeet in the Supreme Court in which it was argued that child prostitutes were living in inhuman conditions and since there is a legislation which empowers the Special Police Officer to rescue such children why no action is taken by the police. This was supported by the signatures of nine child prostitutes who said that they wanted to be rescued. Vishaljeet met Amod Kanth and impressed upon him that the police had the powers even under the Juvenile Justice Act to rescue children. When the raid was made three categories of children were found. A few were child prostitutes, others included children of the prostitutes and child workers in the brothels who worked as domestic workers. When they were rescued it was claimed that all of them were children of the prostituties. Juvenile Welfare Board declared that of the 111 children rescued 97 were not children at all and were released by facial examination. In law there are provisions to determine the age but the Juvenile Welfare Board thought that they could determine the age by seeing the faces and declared that most of the girls were adults and some of them were even mothers. But we know that in India young girls also become mothers before the age of 18. If they are mothers it does not mean that they are not children. This raises a very basic question. What should be done to children in these areas they are children of the prostitutes or whether they are prostitutes themselves? Should they be dealt with under the Juvenile Justice Act or under I.T.P.A.? I think they should be dealt with under the Juvenile Justice Act. Then there is a question whether there should be a right to custody of a prostitute for her child.

There was another petition to the Supreme Court by Gaurav Jain which demanded separate homes and hostels for the children of the prostitutes because their requirements are different. They argued that if they are kept with other children they would not have proper development. Supreme Court did not agree with their petition. A committee was appointed to suggest what should be done in particular for the upliftment of the children of the prostitutes. The Committee studied these Sanskar Ashrams, cottage homes in Delhi and measures adopted all over India and suggested that the children should be kept in homes like those in Delhi. They should not be segragated, nor should they be allowed to stay in the brothels. Prostitute mothers were allowed to visit their children in the Sanskar Ashram once a month, like any other mother, but the days of visit are different so that their identity is not revealed. The contact with mother has not been removed but they have ben removed from the brothels. This I think is very important. The children in these Sanskar Ashrams are below of age of 12 and after that are produced before the Juvenile Department and are then transferred to the Juvenile Homes under the Juvenile Act.

Juvenile Homes some would argue are not the best places to keep the children. But this argument is for all categories of children whether they belong to prostitutes or belong to other categories of neglected children. Juvenile Homes should be improved and they are not the best place but we do not have even a second best option. I think there should be collaboration between the state and the voluntary agencies if we are to improve the conditions of these homes.

We want the legislation to help but what is more important is that we should also know how to use this legislation. What happens is that even if the police knows what the legislation is about and its use, the subjects are unaware of the law. Law is a powerful means of establishing your right, similarly if subjects do not know their rights it can be used to suppress them. People should be made aware of these legislations and the interpretations of the law made which can help them in knowing what their rights are and how to get a redressal for the same.

DISCUSSION

Prof. Lotika Sarkar

I would like to comment on Jean's observation before I open the issue for discussion. While I agree that we should amend I.T.P.A. and take away all penal the provisions, but there is one provision she did not mention but I believe in. I would like you to consider it. There are some of them who live with their families and whose earnings are being used to look after aged parents and young brothers and sisters. But there is, I think a very objectionable provision in the Act which penalises anyone living on the earnings of the prostitutes. I would like you to consider it because if a sex worker wishes to lead a normal life by living with a family why shouldn't she and why should she not maintain her aged parents or brothers and sisters.

Alok Srivastava, Yaar, New Delhi

Prostitution will be a human necessity as long as sex is regulated. That women are the receiving end is only incidental because men have all the purchasing power. When women have purchasing power we will have more and more men into prostitution. Why don't we ask the prostitutes what they want? We need to make distinction between traffcking and wilful sex work. Experience in the West has shown that there will always be women who choose to be in prostitution because that is what they want to do.

Vijay thakur, Hyderabad.

I would just like to ask a question from the speakers and everyone else who are going to debate on this issue. Can we involve women involved in the profession to talk about the problems they have faced during their lifespan due to these laws. Can we set up a national process and them think about it, rather first taking an ideological position. Let us begin with women's voice and group discussions. The women from North Karnataka might want a different law from the women in Andhra Pradesh.

Jean D'Cunha

A very crucial problem that faced us in this whole question is that women who will be active in prostitution cannot get out of it because you cannot offer alternatives immediately in the short run. Women who are working with women in prostitution said that they did not want to work with the third party management system or under the brothel people. Since alternate jobs could not be offered to them, could there be collectives of women working together.

This is an interim measure which was articulated by women in prostitution. However one does not know how good that would work and the kind of problems that it would run into.

Mohini Giri

I am happy to inform you that the National Commission for Women has now formulated a project where the women could themselves form co-operatives. Two acres of land have been given in Andhra Pradesh where they are doing horticulture. We have also tied up with a marketing agency outside for the produce to be sold in temples. Initially entrepreneurial skills will be given to them. If this pilot project works then it could perhaps be introduced elsewhere with help of the NGOs.

Elizabeth, Vatsyan, AAG

I am getting a little uncomfortable hearing the things right now. I sense that we are dying to ghettoise these women, putting them away, putting down collectives, etc. I would like a clarification.

Lalitha S.A., JWP

I would like to inform you that we have with us a number of women in prostitution from the red light areas as well as devdasis, who would like to know about licensing etc. If you ask them directly whether they want licences they would say yes because they do not want to be harassed by the police. But before the licence they will have to undergo the HIV test, and the age determination test to prove that they are above 18. A number of these women come from the village and they don't have their birth certificate. They will have to get an affidavit from the court. That implies they would have to bribe the lawyers and the court or else they will not get the affidavit. Even the doctor will certify only if he is paid Rs. 10,000 or else he will not give a negative HIV certificate. In today's India when we are talking about preventing prostitution why are we talking about giving licence. When the position of women in India today is so bad whether they are the victims of rape, dowry or sale by deception, why are we not fighting these ills? We should talk about licences only when we fail to check prostitution. Besides the police can always maintain in illegal register by taking regular bribe and allow them to carry on their trade. The doctor can also maintain an illegal register by taking Rs.10,000 and allow them to carry on with the trade.

Shyamala Natraj, Madras

I am working in Madras with the South India AIDS Action Programme. These women are today facing the problem of HIV. We have talked about their economic position and social problems but on top of all these problems is the HIV problem. We are talking about licensing, checking of prostitution etc. These are good topics for discusion and that too is necessary but what is actually happening to these women in the last five years in Karnataka, Andhra, Tamil Nadu, Kerala, Maharashtra? We have been a witness to this because we have been working with some of them. The police violence on these women has increased. Five years back this was not an extreme problem. A fortnight ago at Tandivalum 200 kms from Madras in Tamil Nadu, women were dragged from their houses were burnt. When we asked the police why this was done we were told that we should not speak on their behalf becuase they are the cause of the spread of AIDS and so they must in fact be killed. AIDS has become the cause of the increase in violence. We must look into this matter.

As Mr. Srivastava said that it would become very difficult for these women to protect themselves against police violence. What we can do right away is to see that women are not penalised as individuals. In 1991 I fought a case in the Madras High Court. The evidence showed that out of 843 convictions for trafficking offences, one was that of the trafficker.

I feel that the most important thing that these women need to protect themselves is the free Nirodh they receive from the Government. We are in contact with about 15 to 20 thousand women and we were supplying these condoms to them free of cost. The Government under the influence of international agencies like the WHO decided after 40 years to stop supply of free condoms to them. Today the incidence of HIV is high and condoms are the safest means for protection. In a situation like this the Governmennt today has decided to stop completely the supply of condoms which means killing all these women in one shot. Can we do something about this, please?

Ms. Jyotsna Chatterjee

I would say that we should take a stand on this in the next session dealing with health and pass a resolution to this effect.

Jean D' Cunha

I have been asked to repeat the amendments in ITPA

1. One of the suggestions that was made was that with the deletion of Sections 7(1) and 8(b) that is soliciting and practice of prostitution in a public place where women are overwhelmingly being criminalised.

2. A legal provision for the constitution of citizens' committees that will work with the police to track down racketeers, go on raids and follow up prosecution, etc.

3. Advisory Boards in Protective Homes must be constituted.

4. Premoval of discretionary powers to magistrate.

5. Rehabilitation must be in terms of removal of this whole corrective reformative orientation.

6. Addressing the whole issue of prevention in terms of economic and social policy, and cultural question.

7. Removal of a prostitute from a particular place which violates her rights. That section should also be deleted.

8. Gender sensitisation programmes for all govt. personnel.

Dr. Suhasini Subrahamanium, Lady Irwin College.

The chairperson pointed out that may be we should not put a ban on people who are sex worker for the specific reason that they are supporting their families. I have no problem when the sex workers are supporting their aged parents but we have cases of communities such as the Nats and Bedias in Rajasthan where the brother sits back and the sisters work to support the families. In a sense this is exploitation which we will perpetuate in the name of allowing the women to do what they want.

Prof. Lotika Sarkar

There would be cases like that. Why only brothers even the pimps are doing that. All I am saying is that this section rules out everybody - aged parents, brothers, sisters. That is what I objected to. Any judge with sense would see how women are being exploited. I strongly feel that it is wrong to deny her the family life.

Dr. Ved Kumari

I would add that those who would like to use the law to tell them that in the case of Vishal Jeet there are a number of direction given by the Court which can be used by you to pressurise local Governments for setting up of the Advisory Boards.

K.J. Prasad (SALT, Hyderabad)

I am just wondering how it is possible to eliminate police from prevention of immoral traffic. Can we make it a matter of the dept. of social welfare or the department women and child development. Recently, in our state consultation, women in prostitution from 14 districts gathered for the first time. They had been threatened that if they attended this meeting they would be put behind bars. Despite the DSP's assurance, when they attended the meeting and returned they were arrested and each woman had to pay Rs.500 penalty.

If you want to end this evil you must remember that at some stage the aged prostitutes who are becoming house madams should be rehabilitated immediately otherwise the problem continues.

Ajit Singh (Gudia - Varanasi)

On the legalisation issue also I would like to say something. When the police or doctors have not been given legal sanction they still interfere and harass these women. once you legalise the profession their harassment will increase. Right now they are the self appointed guardians when you legalise the profession, the harassment and torture that these women face is also legalised.

4. HEALTH PROBLEMS OF WOMEN IN PROSTITUTION

Discussion were held on the health concerns of women in prostitution in this session that was chaired by Dr. Mira Shiva of the Voluntary Health Association of India. The resource person was Dr. Punit Bedi, gynaecologist.

Jyotsna Chatterji

We now start our next session and the last for the day. This session is on ''Health Problems of Women in Prostitution''. We have with us Dr. Mira Shiva from VHAI. Mira has been a strong supporter of the women's cause in the area of health and we are happy that she is here to chair this session.

Dr. Mira Shiva

I should first acknowledge the fact that my knowledge of all this came after my medical education. If I look back and see how much of this is taught to us even in community medicine or gynaecology the first statement I would like to make is that we are totally unequipped in white coats.

1. My concern is the fact that one gender has a right to sexual pleasure at the cost of anything whether inside the house or outside. Putting on a condom or not putting on a condom is also the right of the male gender.

2. How do we define the reproductive health care and why is it that reproductive health care centres only around women's tubes? Why does not reproductive health care take into account the reproductive and sexual behaviour of

the other gender. Today so much money is being poured into AIDS, reproductive helath care and family planning. All of it is targeted at women. All these things are happening because the sexual behaviour of a certain gender is getting less and less questioned. We are always discussing about the physical health of women but what goes on in the minds of these women is always overlooked. With this I will now ask Dr. Punit to make his presentation.

Dr. Punit Bedi

I am a gynaecologist by training and experience. At the outset I would say that my only experience of treating women who are in prostitution is from my experience of eight years in the gynaecology department of LNJP Hospital which is the closest recognised hospital to Delhi's red light area. If I were to summarise my experience about the health of these women I would say that they require care in three forms.

One is primary health care that any person would require for coughs, cold etc. They have a limited approach to a primary centre or to a general physician.

The second aspect of their health care would be their reproductive health care. In case of prostitutes who become pregnant it becomes a handicap in the profession because there is no family support to fall back upon. There is nobody to take you to the doctor for prenatal care. So there is a peculiar problem of contraception.

So, the first is primary health, second the reproductive health and thirdly there are certain areas which I would like to state are peculiar to these women specially because of their profession. I would like to stress that for these women even when they are suffering from cold it is difficult to approach a doctor. They get fleeced and have to hear a sermon from the doctor instead of getting a simple aspirin.

Of course I don't need to tell you about the backgrounds that these women come from and their educational and personal knowledge of contraception. Contraception for them has quite a different meaning. For them it is a basic essentiality. We all know that once they conceive and have children they face problems. Contraception also has a different meaning with the spread of HIV. Co-operation from customers in the use of condoms is really expecting too much from somebody who is paying for sex.

The third thing that I have been asked to speak on is the peculiar problems that we have today. In this country Government health care is almost always not available to them. They cannot go to a Government hospital and say that I am a prostitute and that I have pelvic infection, please treat it. Nobody will touch her or even take her blood pressure. Most of them get treated by a set of physicians who are in the area. Only in the cases of life and death do they reach the hospital.

There was a young girl who came and complained of serious vaginal bleeding with no pulse and blood pressure, hardly any blood was left in her body. She was probably bleeding for a day and a half already before she came to the hospital. Considering the fact that the hospital is less than a half a kilometre from where she lives this is strange. The people who came gave all sort of stories that she fell across the bicycle seat or a rod accidentally passed through her vagina. It was obvious to me that here was a young girl and somebody had violent sex with her. She had vaginal tear with injuries reaching right up to intestines. In any other circumtance she would have got some treatment. We get these types of tears in newly married girls for various reasons and generally they go to the doctor and the whole story is over. Now she could not get to the right doctor because she could not relate the right history.

What I would like to share with you is that in a hospital like that, any number of women come, who require blood. When we ask for blood we get all kinds of excuses. Even if we tell them that your wife will die the husband generally says that let her die but I will not die with her by giving blood. But in this particular girl case at least 16 people from her brothel donated blood. That enabled the hospital doctors to work on the case. She was in the hospital for a month, underwent an operation and has survived.

The most important infection that they suffer from is the pelvic infection. In the name of AIDS we seem to have forgotten millions of other diseases that are sexually transmitted, which are commoner and carry as much stigma as AIDS. Most of these women have pelvic pain and discharge almost all through their lives. This also happens to otherwise married women and they too get these infections. Here again these women do not get prompt treatment.

The commonest of them all is herpes. Off and on it keeps appearing and it is contagious. It is wrong to presume that only women in prostitution get it. In this country 10% of the whole population has herpes at some stage or the other. There are infections which may be treated such as Syphilis, Gonorrhoea, etc. All these are easily treatable infections which somehow seem to be losing their importance to AIDS. If any kind of health planning has to be done for these women it must be ensured that these people are confident enough to approach these centres.

Someone said authentically that 20% of the women in red light area suffer from AIDS. I know that it is not even legal to do the test on these women. I do not know who has done and what statistics are these. Anyone who gets a grant goes there, tests a few of them and publishes these figures. Press is enthusiastic about figures and the newspapers I see everyday are full of them. Nobody has ever published the percentage of MPs having AIDS or what percentage of doctors, or suburban housewives have it, who are certainly as vulnerable as anybody else being tested. Women in red light areas speading AIDS is a ridiculous statement.

In the last 5000 years we started with leprosy and went on to syphilis, then to plague and we know the panic that was created when 16 cases of plague were reported in this country. Whenever a new infection has come to light the response has always been the same. The easiest thing for the middle class family to accept is that AIDS will affect everyone except him or her. This attitute prevails all over the world. The neighbours burnt the house of a person suspected of AIDS in the USA. This also happened 2000 years ago when people burnt house of those suspected of leprosy.

We all know that high risk behaviour is a very good way of transmittimg AIDS, and the only way of preventing it is a condom. The greatest difficulty in the red light areas is to get good condom and to ensure it is use. As I said it is impossible to ensure its use because we are dependent on the customer. If the women insists that she will not have intercourse without it I don't know how far she can manage that. A much wider programme of making good quality condoms available to everyone not just in red light areas is required. The only significant difference that I have seen between the West and our country is that everyone above 15 years of either gender can handle a condom with confidence whether he or she has ever had sex or not. But in this country even a 55 year old cannot use it. This is the only thing however that can prevent AIDS and certainly one thing that will not help is statistics.

Unlike the family system where a woman attracts attention during pregnancy, these women are neglected during the time when they need attention with respect to nutrition, living conditions and medical care. So any organisational support that is given to young children should also be extended to women who are expecting. Some care in the form of nutritional support should be there.

As said at the outset, it is not only sexually transmitted diseases and pregnancy that is neglected but even primary health care is neglected. If a women in prostitution has a pelvic pain everyone will treat her for pelvic infection without considering the possibility that she can also get appendicitis. Considering their economic background they could every well be suffering from TB or respiratory disease because of living in polluted areas. In the given conditions the only thing one can do is to make health care accessible to them.

I would like to add that activities of NGOs are not regulated. There is no way to check the authenticity of their research and information. For example the person who said that 22% people are HIV positive in red light areas, you can't break her head for that statement. What kind of regulation you have? If I say that 90% of the gynaecologist are HIV positive the Association of Gynasecologists can take no action against me. So this kind of irresponsible statements are made. Ironically NGOs have a lot of credibility. Just because the Government is discredited for various reasons. The same information stated by the Health Ministry may spread doubt but if it comes from a well meaning NGO it is believed.

DISCUSSION

Dr. Mira Shiva.

I just want to make a comment on access to health care services. 70 to 80% of the health care service in the country is in private hands. Most of the Government health services are around family planning, immunisation, etc. Family planning again is targeted on women. If you even look at that and its implication on reproductive track infection and HIV it is clear that contraceptives and hormonal operations have an effect on immune systems. As mentioned by Dr. Bedi, putting in an IUD without even preliminary attempt at diagnosing and treating is common practice. There is no budget for basic health services, gynaecological problems but there is enough budget for high-tech stuff. I think availability of condoms should be on top of the agenda.

Then the whole question of violence. The women in this profession commonly experience sexual violence and violence of other kind. Anything that is medico-legal most of the doctors will not touch with the barge pole. Under the consumer Protection Act one of the things that would happen is that anyone who is in serious condition, many of them would not want to touch.

Usha Wagh, Pune

Do children of prostitutes inherit diseases more than children who are from normal women? It is my experience that when we take the prostitute's children to the doctor, as Dr. Punit also said they are not given the same treatment as would be given to normal women when they have pelvic pain. How can activists like us convince the doctor that these children are no different from other women.

Dr. Punit Bedi

Women in Prostitution are not abnormal. Their reproductive system and their children are as normal as others. It would be like saying that doctors lawyers and their children have special abnormalities. If a woman is in prostitution and she has infections which can be transmitted vertically like HIV that cannot be considered inherited abnormality.

Poonam Sahi, National Commission for Women

How can we rope in the private practitioners to be aware of the non-governmental reproductive services. How can we get the private practitioners to be concious about this and to get them into family planning counselling. Since they are such a big chunk of the medical family they should be involved in this or else it is just left to their individual conscience to deliver family planning services.

Dr. Punit Bedi

Actually these issues were never raised because the question of accountability of doctors is never raised. Doctors are getting away with murder. Even today with this so-called Consumer Protection Act, the law has not changed. Accountability is still very difficult. If I put a scalpel in somebody's heart it is almost impossible to hang me even today. These are minor issues which are very important, the society itself has to grow to a level where you can ask your doctor and make him accountable directly or indirectly.

Modern medicine has not provided any relief on the contrary it has created many new problems.

Jean D'Cunha

I want to know experience of the mental health of women in prostitution.

Dr. Punit Bedi

I am afraid I cannot say much about it because mental health as it is a very neglected issue in this country.

I treated some young girls from red light area and they in turn brought more girls for treatment, to the extent that I got the reputation that women from red light areas could get treated in the Government hospital. Then they started coming very easily to me. Being a gynaecologist one has very little chance to sit and chat with them in OPDs. I must say that somebody must do some work on it which I cannot.

Ms. Shanti, Christian Medical Assocaition Of India

I had a chance to work with these women in red light areas. Depression is common among them. Some of them have suicidal tendencies. Depression can be because of their ecoomic condition but most of it is due to lack of family support. They feel that have failed their families.

Ajit Singh, Varanasi

Another thing that I think is important is the feeling that they are sex workers.

Mr. D.S. Rai, Madhya Pradesh

I am from Madhya Pradesh. I will be making a separate statement tomorow. I want to tell you about the situation that preplexes us. I am dealing with some villages which traditionally are the source for prostitution. I have been observing these families for the last few years and have been taking the doctors there. None of them have been found to be suffering from STD and AIDS. They live up to 60 years and are active sex workers from age of 16 to 40 years. They take a lot of non-vegetarian food, drink heavily and take on 8 to 10 customers on an average per day. It preplexes me now that they have not fallen prey to STDs. Can you enlighten us?

Dr. Mira Shiva

We cannot comment on that because at times those who performs tests say that the women do not suffer from AIDS. So how are they examined and who examines them, is to be taken in to account. I will not comment on that but may be because of good food and economic strength that they lead healthy lives.

Subir Bannerjee, Calcutta

As a gynaecologist have you experienced any difference in the manner of expressing the problems by women from red light areas and housewives. I think there is higher degree of consciousness in women from red light areas about their gynaecological problems. This is relevant because I think women form red light area maintain a different culture and those from so called civilised families have a different lifestyle.

Dr. Punit Bedi

I believe that these are more economic than really educational problems. If I were to compare these women with similar families with same economic background I think there is not much difference. Lately women from red light areas seem to have heard of AIDS but it is not that they are taking more precautions than others.

In no way would they come and say that they are from the red light areas. It is because have been working in groups for long we know that they are from that area.However I do manage to get out a lot of information, once a rapport is built they are quite honest and frank about their problems. That is for both the groups whether in prostitution or otherwise.

K.J. Prasad, Hyderabad

My whole question is about the confidentiality and acceptance of women in prostitution in the institution of medical services. We see that their accessibility is to the quacks or RMPs but not with the primary health centes or any Government hospitals because of this overemphasis on relationship of HIV/AIDS with prostitutes.

To be specific, three years back in Hyderabad, a medical doctor from a Government hospital casually said that in Mehendi there are three women who are HIV Positive, the net result was that all 300 women living in that area were removed from their houses for 15 days and exposed to the dust & heat with children. That is the terror created in the name of HIV / AIDS. When we talk about the health services accessibility the nearest persons for them are the quacks or native practitoners. We should think in these terms because most of the women are not urban centered but also operational in rural areas, specially around the highway tracks. When you travel by road you can see the drivers stopping on the way and picking up girls. It is a big racket that is going on the national highways. For such women there is no accessibility to the health centres .

Shyamala Nataraj, Madras

It is true, women, whether they belong to prostitution or not, have problems regarding accessibility to health services. We however have an experience to share with you which you could probably adopt. Whether we like it not we do have Government services which are provided for. They may not be the best but by interventions they can be made to function effectively. In any case the vast mass of people have to be dependent on these services.

Our experience has been with the STD department of a hospital where we have a trained counsellor from the side of NGOs, who sits in the STD department of the hospital. We find that during the last two and a half years the quality of service in the department has improved a lot and many women in prostitution who used to visit the quacks today are now coming to this hospital because they are able to meet the counsellor who makes them feel comfortable. The counsellor has also influenced the set up in the clinic so that there is more privacy, confidentiality and sensitivity. This has not only happened with women in prostitution but it has also happened to the general population. We find that more people are bringing their partners for treatment at the hospital, which is very important if you do not want reinfection, and at the STD clinics itself the doctors when they are prescribing medicines with the treatment they also precribe condoms. This counsellor distributes the condoms with the message that it can be used to prevent infection, and shows them how to use it. It has been a very good experience in limited way.

Dr. Punit Bedi

Eventually we have found the issue is not what diseases these people have or any women has and what treatment we are providing, The issue is that time and again the medical profession has failed to deliver the basic thing that they exist for. Why a woman who is in prostitution cannot go and get treatment in the hospital just like any other woman is a question that will be raised again and again. In all cases it is the primary ethical question for the doctor. Very conveniently the Government hospitals have been excluded from the Consumer Protection Act even in the Supreme Court judgement. There is no legal or logical medical reasons for excluding Government hospitals from basic accountability. An average person is more likely to be abused in these centres than in any other place. More than health awareness and accessibility we should be talking about the accountability of doctors and we should pass a resolution in this meeting to that effect.

Mr. B.L. Patil, Karnataka

We are working in Vimochana, Athni, Karnataka. We organised an AIDS detection camp in 1985 with 30 devadasi women with whom we were working. The camp was conducted by one of the eminent pathologists of the contry. In those days if was one of the biggest AIDS camps in Karnataka. Fortunately none of these women were HIV positive.

In 1989 we conducted another AIDS detection camp when we were working with 700 women, 16 positive cases were reported. Then we held a meeting of our sisters and consulted them as to what should be done. That is the procedure followed by us. We do not take a decision on our own but let the women take decisions. They suggested that don't publish the results of the test and make us social outcasts. Thereafter no detection camps were conducted. It was their decision. Now we follow a different procedure. Now twice a year we conduct a padyatra where the religious heads of Karnataka are invited and they propogate a campaign on AIDS awareness. Probably that was the first time in the history of the nation that religious heads participated in the AIDS campaign.

Ajit Singh

Before the tests were conducted was there free counselling and when the tests were performed were women aware that they were the tests for AIDS?

B.L. Patil

Doctors from Belgaun were camping there for three days for conducting the tests.

Dr. Punit Bedi

Were they told that why test was being done? Were they given any choice at all?

B.L. Patil

They were told that it was an AIDS detection camp and that they would be thrown out was not told. Out of 300 women, 170 were tested.

Dr. Punit Bedi

How were these 170 selected?

B.L. Patil

There was no selection. 300 were invited but only 170 were present.

Dr. Punit Bedi

That is what we are objecting to. All kings of testing on the population groups has not helped us at all. You have rightly abandoned the programme, it is very sensitive.

Rephael Paulson, Kerala

We would like to raise the issue of drug addiction. It is a legal and as well as health problem, few people have programmes to fight this. For the police it is an easy weapon. They call these people to the police statiion, plant these drugs on them and then charge them to harass them. We had a seminar where a police officer admitted that he picks these women at random from the railway and bus stations and then charges them with possession of drugs.

Dr. Mira Shiva

I know that women in prostitution are induced into drug addiction. This dimension should be discussed. The fact that people are in wrongful confinement for drug addiction is also true and should be taken a seriously. It is not an easy task to deal with this problem.

Vijay Thakur, Hyderabad

We would like to bring to your notice the work of an NGO in Maharashtra and may be you can assess its effectiveness. In Maharashtra 2500 women have been given health cards officially by the Health Ministry which entitles them to free and non-discriminatory access to Government health care. Any complaint arising from the user of this card is processed directly by the Director of Health Services and there are no intermediaries. The NGO is supposed to be a complaint box to route these complaints. This is on trial for the last 4 months.

Dr. Punit Bedi

I would also suggest that all kinds of arbitrary testing. targeting women in prostitution should be stopped immediately. They serve no purpose and I suggest that my colleagues and NGOs should refrain from using alarming statistics of incidents elsewhere. These have not helped in the control of AIDS or any other disease anywhere in the world.

Secondly, what is vital is the accountability of doctors whether it is AIDS or any other disease or providing primary health care for women in prostitution. I think the issue of accountability is very important and strictures should be passed against doctors who refuse treatment to these women.

K.J. Prasad, Hyderabad

I would like to suggest as a resolution could we take on the para medical sector, train them and sensitise them with awareness. We can use them until the registered medical practitioner comes into the picture.

Dr. Punit Bedi

I agree with him because there is no way other doctors are going to the highway dhabas. Whoever is available should be upgraded.

Dr. Mira Shiva

I think that good quality condom distribution should also be emphasised in the resolution.

The question of safe sex means not getting AIDS, violent sex is also safe sex as long as you have the condom on. We require a redefinition of the AIDS messages which are not at all gender sensitive. I feel also there is a need for entire revamping of the OB Gynae teaching in the profession. In the present condition understanding women and the social context is absolutely absent. Even our understanding about the women in prostitution is not taught under Community Health.

Shyamala Nataraj, Madras

Is is possible to frame our resolution with respect to women in prostitution that any violence or discrimination against women in prostitution, is only the visible part of violence and disrimination against all women.

Jyotsna Chatterje

This is acceptable to all.

Dr. Mira Shiva

There is no question about the double standards in society. There is talk about fallen women and not fallen men. Some of these issues need to be looked into more seriously otherwise the attitudes are going to continue.

We will wind up to say that the health problems of women in prostitution are not just of the physical nature but one part of the entire dimension of the social health and mental health which is usually neglected. Unless the social dimension is adequately taken care of ımprovement in physical health will not take place.

Then the availability of condoms should be there in the market.

The entire medical profession and the confidentiality dimension is posing a serious problem for women in prostitution and needs to be looked into seriously. Self help groups in the communities can do a much better job and therefore they should be given priority and training.

Access to basic diagnostic facilities and essential drugs for the commoner, women's trade related health problems, and their access to it should be gi ven a high priority.

In the absence of basic care services, mere AIDS related and reproductive health related vertical programmes are not going to work. One of the demand should be that all programmes must reach rural women.

Dr. Punit Bedi

I had talked about the accountability of the doctors. I would like to add to it the accountability of the press and the NGOs. If somebody brings two HIV Postive persons and exposes them at press conference, they require the same pre-conference counselling as pre testing requires. Even if their consent was implied they are probably not aware of all the consequences. Today the NGOs and the press have become accountable. Just like in rape you can name the rapists and not the victim, in the case of women in prostitution when a doctor refuses to treat her, the doctor's name should be there and not that of a patient.

5.
REHABILITATION AND CONSIDERATION OF VIABLE ALTERNATIVES

This was the penultimate session of the workshop that was presided over by Dr. Sarala Gopalan, Secretary, Department of Women & Child Development.

Dr. Sarala Gopalan, Secretary, Department of Women & Child

Watching you introduce yourselves it was heartening to learn that there are so many organisations who have already recognised these social problems and are working in the area of prevention, rehabilitation, care of the children and awareness generation programmes. I think this is one area where it is very difficult to have exact data because currently the greater concern as Ms Elizabeth Vatsayan mentioned is the spread of AIDS. Recently there was an international seminar on AIDS in Delhi and we read about the problem spreading to the household sector because of the lack of awareness. Unfortunately the sex workers are the major victims. The sharpest action and impact has to be in the prevention not only of AIDS but also prevention of women taking to this profession.

I think there are two distincts terms that have been identified. One is the poverty stream and the other is the traditional stream like the devdasis and others. In most states where the latter practice has been identified laws have been enacted. Only in Orissa there is no law. In Andhra and Karnataka there are laws. Recently I learnt that even in Bihar where "Adithi" is working they have found a community that has a custom similar to devadasi culture. We must go into all these areas and take up poverty alleviation/rehabilitation programmes.

We need to do something more drastic in order to address this problem in a holistic manner. I do not know whether this symposium would be able to marshal enough data so that we can come out with a project. We will have to conduct a multi dimensional exercise.

In the process we will have to attack the mindsets of the people wherever this tradition is accepted and it becomes compulsory for some of these girls in the families to take to this profession.

Another case would be where they are forced into this profession. Many others are lured into it by elements who are trying to make money out of the flesh trade. The action should start where you locate a proneness to these elements.

We need to simultaneously sensitise the administration involved in the implementation of these laws. I look forward to getting useful information from your workshop.

The first stage would be to use the various programmes that we already have for improving income generation activities for women and development of their skills, only you have to package it in a different manner. I am willing to take up area by area. Let us identify the organisations that are working there, what is the networking that is required to be done, so that whatever resources we have are not frittered away due to ignorance. I think you have to make a project to take care of the adolescent girls, so that at least the next generation would be rehabilitated. Those who have already become victims we have to think very seriously about their rehabilitation problem.

Much literature will have to be generated on the various alternatives which can be pursued. This has to be done carefully because it is difficult to penetrate into the complexities of society in order to identify who is more prone to them.

What needs to be done is to take up an area, identify the group of persons who need to be covered and according to their status, their educational skill levels, the geographical position of that place, decide on the feasability of taking up the project for them. If we do that exercise and prepare a master micro plan for that area I think we will be able to tackle that problem intelligently.

I hope you will come out with a practical action plan. Even if we take up a detailed study to make this action plan it would be worthwhile doing the study. We need to tackle this in a systematic manner. Let us find out the areas where the intensity of the problem is greater and make out a programme of action for each of these areas, identify the organisation who will take it up and review all programmes to tackle this. We used the ICDS Adolescent Girls Programme to find the number of adolescent girls coming to ICDS centres which are almost universal now. 70% of the blocks are covered by that. There are various other awareness generation, vocational training courses of the Central Social Welfare Board.

I think it is important that we do the whole work in a more systematic manner. Networking among organisation that are all working in this field is vital. Let there be information exchange. If we act in that manner we might be able to reach somewhere. It is easy for me to say this but I am aware that it is not easy to translate into action. But when you desegregate and start planning carefully, the most difficult thing can be achieved.

Mr. Gerry Pinto, UNICEF India

.There are a number of experienced participants around this table. I am a student who is here to learn. I am not an expert on the subject because there is very little that I have done in terms of action on this subject. It is in the context of understanding the problem that we have been participating and supporting these meetings to come to an understanding of what are the real dimensions and the issues relating to the problem.

The issue of children as a vulnerable group is no more an option for social welfare. It is more a moral and legal compulsion, particularly when 178 countries including India have ratified the Convention for the Rights of the Child. I think for too long one has looked at children as beneficiaries of welfare and philanthropy. The mind set of the people concerned should be changed first to look at children not as passive recipients of charity and social welfare.

The issue of child prostitution is not an issue of the department or of the Government. Unless we project this issue as an issue of society I think we can go a very limited way. Having a project or interventions are necessary but if we limit our sensitivity only to that level, we are limiting ourselves from the very beginning regarding understanding the nature of the problem. It is important and people have made reference to the network that exists which perpetuates the problem. If we have to talk about starting action we need to identify these networks and address them.

One of the critical interventions that must be in the direction of greater efforts at mobilisation, creating community awareness and empowerment of women. When girls are not treated as equals even as children there is no way women would be treated as equal to men. If we have to create sensitivity towards the issue of child prostitution or girl child abuse, we have to begin way down from childhod.

The next area, which has been discussed here to some extent, is the media. At various meetings the destruction caused by the media is discussed It is important to look at how media can be an important ally and not an enemy who we have to keep fighting. How does media project girls and women? Do they really project women as empowered human beings of society? We need to address that if the media has to become an ally in our efforts towards addressing this issue.

Promoting education, particularly enrolling of girls, addressing the issue of female drop outs from primary schools, in particular, can be a very substantial direction of prevention. But that is very simply said. How do we make education meaningful for girls? It is just not forcing girls to join the schools, it is an obligation even of the school system to ensure that schools are meaningful. Human rights is part of the title of the workshop. Human rights can never be addressed unless you address the rights of women and children who form the major part of the society.

We are talking more and more about the growing importance of panchayats. How do we put this issue on the agenda of panchayats? Children in prostitution is a community issue and it has to be taken seriously and acted upon by people who represent the community particularly at the village level. We need to build a strong working alliance with the representatives of people and not operate on this programme as a social welfare scheme away from the representatives of people. References have been made to the source districts. If there has to be a long term impact on the problem it is very important to identify those areas which are perpetually sending children to be fed into this industry. I know that at the micro level some NGOs are looking at this issue but I think there has to be a more organised way of focusing on areas that are responsible for generating children for this profession.

There is a tendency to look at the whole issue of child prostitution as a child welfare related problem. Can we take the action of promoting advocacy with women's groups that as part of women's concern this issue should form part of their agenda.

I think people have mentioned that rehabilitation may not be a priority in the long term perspective but there is no way we can get away from it if we have to look at children who are already engaged in this or trapped in this vulnerable situation. I am sure that people who have tried it can tell us stories of frustration - how the issue of children in prostitution cannot be easily addressed by rehabilitation. I am aware that institutionalisation approach has been a popular approach but unfortunately this target group has very different features as compared to other target groups, whether they are orphans or neglected children, delinquent children, abandoned children, street children or child labour. Traditional social welfare approaches that emphasise institutional care would definitely have limitations. At the same time special programmes for children in prostitution may not be a very positive solution.

The problem must be assessed within the socio-economic parameters and the approaches to rehabilitation necessarily have to be holistic. In that sense I would try to put the idea that the problem of children in prostitution is not the problem of children. Unless you look at the problem as the problem of families, problem of vulnerable groups, problem of marginal class groups, etc., you can not address the problem in a substantial way. People do say that the problem of prostitution is a historical one and sometimes people even wonder whether the best approach is to legalise it. I am not getting into that debate but all of us are unanimous that where children are concerned there is no excuse.

These days we hear about publications like the Progress of the Nations, where countries have been listed in terms of progress on the indicators relating to child health, mortality, morbidity, etc. I would feel that there should be one single indicator which should be most critical in judging a nation whether there is progress in the status of the girl child. If one can arrive at the number of children being forced into prostitution, that one indicator will tell us about the level of progress of the community.

The other dimension when we talk about children in prostitution in India is that we have to look at it as a problem of the region because it involves trafficking across the borders of the country. It is very encouraging to note that the whole subject broadly described as "girls in difficult circumstances" with a clear emphasis on child prostitution, has been put on the agenda of the SAARC countries. In the Colombo meeting held in early November there was a commitment to look at the issue in the joint forum of the SAARC so that trafficking can be addressed by collaborative efforts among these neighbouring countries.

I had made a point in my paper about the alliance between the police and the NGOs. There was a Police Commissioner in Bombay who participated in the national consultation on prostitution last year. He made an interesting presentation. He said many of us seem to pride ourselves with the number of raids we conduct and the number of children released. It is a hollow pride because the process is well known. The children are released temporarily from bondage and prostitution. Only to be fed back into the system. He was basically making an appeal to the NGOs who would be willing to be partners with the police particularly to address the next step. Releasing the children is the first step and it can be sometimes done in a sensitive way and sometimes in a non sensitive way. The issue really is what happens to the child once the child is released. Can there be a forum of NGOs and interested people who would take on the role not on their own but with support from the State Governments. No rehabilitation programmes are sustainable unless they are based on the community. Can there be ways of building on community initiative?

I had an opportunity to visit a project in North Arcot District which is run on the initiative of the Collector and his team with the support of the community. There they are identifying communities and families who have children working as bonded labourers and targeting these families with poverty alleviation programmes and income generation activites including credit facilities. Women are given a loan of Rs. 10 to Rs.15,000, part of which they pay to the person who holds them in bondage and the remaining is invested in milch cow. Consequently earnings per day of the woman is Rs. 40 a day. I think the principle that is operating there is not to create special development programmes to address issues of child prostitution. The Collector was very insistent that to address the problem of child labour they do not require another programme. What is needed is motivating the departments which have got various programmes and get them to target on these families so that poverty is reduced and they do not have the pressure of living on the income of the child.

People have said that the major cause of child prositution and many other problems is poverty. I do not think that we can negate that. The question is that do all poor families send their chilren to prostitution? This is to clarify our thinking and not to argue or take a particular stand. I think poverty plus other factors that coincide, relating to religious beliefs or cultural practices can push children to prostitution. While poverty might be a major cause we have to be sensitive to other factors that make the families more vulnerable.

Jyotsna ji told me in the beginning that the idea was to address the projects to the problems. The encouraging part she told me was that the projects would be for the prevention. Can we arrive at some packages and interventions which can demonstrate that if the intervention is focused on a clearly defined area there can be some prevention. We also have to ask ourselves whether we really want to perpetuate this label which isolates them further rather than help them to come to the mainstream. The attention seems to be going on the second word, labour and prostitution, not so much on the 'child'. I think the beginning of all effective programmes is when they are based on the needs of children as children.

Sometimes the disability of the society is transferred in labelling. The classic example is the term "illegitimate children". It is difficult to find out who is illegitimate. Even about delinquent children one does not know whether society and the country is delinquent or the children. Similarly in child prostitution, I think the attention should be more on the fact that they are children who need our attention on a priority basis.

In many parts of the world child prostitution has been seen as part as an extreme form of hazardous child labour. There is an interesting angle to that. We look at strategies that are being supported these days to address the problem of elimination of child labour and see within the same principles and approaches, strategies which could be included to address the problem of child prostitution.

Shri D.S. Rai, Distt. Raisen, Madhya Pradesh

I must admit at the outset that my experience in this field is far limited than what is being done by all of you in this field. My experience is limited to one year or so.

The Literacy Campaign has been a very important instrument to bring about social change. In Raisen district, for example, it was only through the literacy campaign that we could approach the 4.5 lakh women in the district.

Bedini or Bedias are a community that is a reserved caste, and were earlier included in the Scheduled Caste list. The total number of Bedini families in Madhya Pradesh is about 70,000, spread over 15 districts. No authentic history of the community is known but interestingly they were the people who about 200 years ago would brew liquor and commit dacoities for the small kings. When the Britishers came down heavily on them the dacoities stopped and they had no other way but to fall back on cheaper and easier methods of earning money. One of them was to provide entertainment by singing and dancing. This also resulted in their taking up prostitution and becoming concubines of the big people in the late 19th century. By the end of the last century they had fallen to the profession of prostitution.

Any woman who sings, dances and is a prostitute is called a Bedini, but the wife of the Bed man is not a Bedini. Any woman who is married will never engage in prostitution. She is engaged in prostitution as long as she is not married. Any daughter can be a Bedini, but once married she stops prostitution and becomes a respectable mother. But this happens to only 30% of the women.

As a result of this in my district where I am working there are about 150 families,where girls and daughters are actively engaged in dancing and singing. They perform a powerful dance form of Bundelkhand which is known as Rai. It is performed for the monied people of the village when there is a marriage or when a child is born. The group can consist of 8 to 10 people, one or two are girls, and the rest are dholak players, flute players, etc. The cost of each programme is two to three thousand. After the programme the Bedini girl makes the night for the man who calls her to perform.

Interestingly enough, the father is never shy of sending his daughter to the profession may be because the father is himself not very sure that he is the real father of the girl. The brother never feels shy that he is making use of the money his sister is bringing because in reality the sister may not be from the same father.

It is interesting that despite all the abuse they are engaged in, the Bedini women have not been found to be victims of AIDS or STDs. We have doctors visiting them every week and we get condoms distributed freely. The general complaint is that the people who come to them do not prefer condoms. The reason for their not having bad health may be because they eat well. They earn a lot of money, drink heavily and eat non vegetarian food regularly till the time they are in the earning age. The earning age starts from 13 to 14 years and lasts up to 40 years.

We started our Literacy Campaign on 1 July, 1994. We also wanted to tell the women about their rights. We organised several fronts for women based on their needs/background. One was the Mahila Samta Manch, which covers all women of any age. Mahila Samta Manch has been given a concrete course of action and in my district which has 14289 villages, we have been able to make 1300 Mahila Samta Manch. The voluntary trainers teaching the literacy classes are the secretary or president of the Mahila Samta Manch. This is because the usual panch, unless she is trained further or empowered, will not come to organise the meeting of the Mahila Manch. The trainers of literacy campaigns who have been selfless workers have immediately come forward.

For the Muslim women we have a Progressive Muslim Women's Front. To catch the girls young and to let them know about their rights we started Nari Shakti Vahini covering all girls above 14 years of age till they are married. Nari Shakti Vahini functions in all the schools. For prostitutes, women who have been deserted by their husbands, divorcees, spinsters for all such women we started Akela Angan Mahila Sangh.

Through these four fronts we were able to approach the women at all possible levels, right from 13 years to 70 years. We soon got to know that in our district of Raisen with a population of 9 lakhs there were at least 5000 ladies who had been deserted by their husbands without giving them any maintenance allowance. Men have married for the second time sending the first wife home and there are 5000 women living with their parents with no income and may be with a small child as an added burden. Again there are 5000 widows who are in the marriageable age of 20 to 35. Remarriage of widows is very uncommon.

The existence of prostitutes in the Bedia community in the three villages of the district came to our knowledge in August 1994. I made them one promise that if some of them left prostitution forever we would try to help them from the

Government. Coming to an emotional level I promised them that I would make them my sister by getting the rakhi string if they left prostitution. On the rakhi day of 1995 I went back to these villages and the women who had left prostitution tied the 'rakhi' on my wrist. As you know 'Rakhi' is considered a very auspicious symbol for Hindu women. The gesture made them very happy and they have become our active workers. Thus began the community initiative. The women who left prostitution are now with the Government, helping us to further motivate other women to come out of profession with their cooperation. We have been able to make inroads into the community of prostitutes in the two villages.

We have also tackled the problem at the emotional level. My daughter is sixteen years of age. The sixteen year old daughters of these women are about to be initiated into prostitution. I took my own daughter to these villages and showed them how education is important for the girl child. When you take your own daughter forgetting that it is a forbidden area, the emotional gesture has an impact. They now call me Bhaisahib and ask me to intervene if a new girl is being initiated for a dance.

As far as the help from the Government is concerned all such women have been taken for training under TRYSEM and those who completed training under TRYSEM for 'duree making' have been given loans under the IRDP. The Government of Madhya Pradesh has started a novel scheme of providing housing to all those who are homeless. My proposal to the Secretary is that by a special order some agricultural land may be kept reserved for allotment to the families that traditionally send their girls into prostitution.

Another thing that we did was to target the young boys. They start working as a pimp by the time they are 15 years old for their own sister. Far more important therefore is education for these boys. This year we took 100 boys from two villages and sent them to various boys' hostels all over the district. I have 47 hostels in the district and I adjusted 4 to 5 in each hostel. Initially they wanted to run away and come back home because there was more discipline. But 90% of them have stayed back in the hostels.

A very important suggestion was made yesterday. Though the panchayats in Madhya Pradesh are responsible for the supervision of almost all rural activities including activities of rural child and welfare departments, working for the betterment of the prostitutes is something which should be put on the agenda of the panchayats. The panchayat of specific villages should be given extra money, send a weekly report and if a girl is initiated into prostitution the panchayat should also be held partly responsible.

I must give credit to the women folk of the district who have come forward in a big way. In most of the meetings the percentage of women present is almost two times the percentage of men. We have been able to to locate 20 such women among the Bedinis. We know that results would take a long time to come because of the easy money that comes out of prostitution is not going to come out of cultivation. They get 10 customers a day at the rate of Rs. 30 to 200 and they earn about Rs. 2000 per day. This money cannot come from grazing or cultivation. So this is going to take some time. But we are hopeful that with the help of the women of Raisen and NGOs we are going to be successful.

DISCUSSION

Dr. Sarla Gopalan

I can give you an example of another experiment. In Tanjore district one voluntary organisation took up the programe of land redistribution. They have used their IRDP programme. These families were all scheduled castes. Unlike in Madhya Pradesh, in Tamil Nadu and most part of South India the per capita land holding is very small and the ceiling for individual holding is very small. You cannot hold more than seven acres of irrigated land. What this voluntary organisation did was to identify some people who wanted to sell their land because they could not cultivate. They bought almost thousand acres of land using the IRDP money and distributed it through the Schedule Caste and Scheduled Tribes Corporation by giving the land through 50% loan and 50% subsidy from IRDP. They did not give the whole amount in one go but in three or four batches. 50% came from the subsidy of IRDP and 50% from SC / ST Corporation loan. Then they identified 100 landless families belonging to SC & ST, gave them one hectare with a commitment that 50% of the loan has to be paid back.

I was called to give them suggestions about how to use the land. We called the district administration and all the development officers and identified all their schemes. We found that in the district there are a number of schemes on irrigation particularly on minor irrigation, for Scheduled Castes & Scheduled Tribes. In these schemes 50% subsidy is available and 50% is loan but initially 100% comes from under the scheme. Similarly for the land development there are other schemes. So we tried to identify all these schemes and projectise them so that they get the benefit of the subsidy. We found that we could have loans for everything, building a house, dig canals and wells, buy the implements, etc. Each family requires Rs. 50,000 loan and 50% you receive as subsidy. In other words with one lakh you liberate the family from poverty for all time.

K.J. Prasad, SALT, Hyderabad

In Andhra Pradesh we experimented with one programme. When a house is given to the economically weaker section it is given as joint ownership and on the condition that it is the husband who leaves the house and not the wife. That is the legislation there. That is a cue you can take because in most of these cases maintenance cannot be obtained because they are not having any property or any Government service Shelter is most important.

We have traditional prostitution among Venkatasanis in our state who are coming fom the Domara community. Our main problem is with the community heads. They are even threatening the police. To quote one example, in Warangal district where we tried to stop the dedication and initiation into prostitution, the Superintendents of Police were transferred within a month. How are the community heads responding to your action, may be because you are a Collector you are heeded. We are NGO nobody listens to us.

Mr D. S. Rai

Fortunately for us in Raisen there are no community heads as such for the Bedia community. There is an elderly woman who is supposed to be a leader. She was herself in prostitution and is now away from it. But it is not necessary that her direction or voice is heard by everybody. We do not have to tackle any community heads for the moment and we are trying to tackle them individually.

Elizabeth Vatsyan, AIDS Action Group

I would like to respond to what Mr Rai has been saying. I would say that you are on the right track and that you have done some very positive work which is commendable. However there are certain points about which I which I felt uncomfortable. You talked about compulsory taking away of children, especially girls and putting them in schools. Your intentions are very good but this whole business of compulsory taking away children from their mothers smacks very much of what happened in 1988 about which all of us are very angry up to date.

Mr D.S. Rai

I apologise. I must verify that by taking them compulsorily did not mean that they have been dragged out. The consent of mothers was taken.

Elizabeth Vatsyan

This should be on record because otherwise it gives a wrong impression. Otherwise it would have been the same as what Mr Amod Kanth had done.

Mr. D.S. Rai

I must make it clear that it was not forcible. They gave their written consent. But this was made compulsory after we had convinced them. It was not by police action that we took children out. There was no punishment involved. No force was used and no punishment was shown. It was through motivation and not in Amod Kanth's style.

Let me inform you one more thing about the campaign. Literacy campaign does not mean only 'Akshar Gyan'. We have taught the neo literates that after being literate you should become aware of your rights and know how you were being discriminated against and also who is responsible for that discrimination. Literacy campaign is successful only if people realise their rights. In the last one year and a half we have distributed literature which is in their interest. The objective is to make them socially conscious and also make them realise that they have to move forward and fight injustice.

Q. J. Zaidi, Hyderabad

From my experience in Uttar Pradesh. I can tell you that there are very few NGOs who are working in this field, who are recipients of any Government support and help. NGOs which exist on paper get all support and they are able to get as many as 25 to 30 projects simultaneously.

Once a team from Tata Institute of Social Sciences came and asked if there were any recognised organisations which were working in this field. We told them to go and find out for themselves. They could not find even two organisations. They said that there are only Short Stay Homes set up by the Social

Welfare Boards. We said go and find out for yourself. When they visited Collector's office they were told by his secretary not to ask for the file as that would create a problem. This is the set up that we are working in.

Shyamala Nataraj, Madras

In Tamil Nadu we adopted 17 women from the Bombay red light area. When we started giving them some kind of training, three or four women left us and the re-entered the same profession.

I personally feel that your scheme is successful there because it is a tribal belt and also you are sitting like a big brother who can handle the situation. My experience reveals that people of different communities put pressure on them to continue in the same profession.

Mr. D.S. Rai

It is correct that not all poor girls enter prostitution. The Bedia community has no pride in its own history. For hundred years they have been engaged in this profession. But the cobbler community have not entered this profession even in the poorest situations. So it depends on the community.

In Delhi as was rightly said, the cause for alarm is that prostitution may be a source for generating income in urban centres. I was in DDA during 1992-93 and I have the experience that thousands of girls and women are operating in Delhi. This is easy money when they come to it by their own choice.

Subir Bannerjee, Calcutta

I think that you are more of a social worker than an administrator. You have motivated the community but in our State matter of motivation of the community is very difficult. If the prostitute returns to her original home, if other people come to know of her profession, she will not be allowed to stay there. How did you really motivate them, what were the methods you adopted?

Mr. D. S. Rai

Again I must give all credit to the womenfolk who are much more responsive to social problems than men. We have not been able to mobilise the men as much as women. My wife and other ladies visit the village, stay there and discuss problems with ex-prostitutes. Women understand the problem of women more easily. What it is like to be a prostitute can be understood better by a woman than by the man. So the response of the female community is much more important than the response of the male community.

Mr. S. K. Guha

I think what Mr Rai said about using religious examples as means of communication can very useful. He has not made any value judgement about any particular religious prescription. He has only said that religious anecdotes and instances can be effective in communication.

I think one difference between the type of situation that Mr Rai spoke of and the kind of situation that you face in Allahabad, Delhi, Bombay or Calcutta is that the form of prostitution which he spoke of had a very strong cultural orientation. The type of mobilisation that you can do in the village is quite different from he type of mobilisation that you can attempt to do in the red light areas of Bombay or Calcutta. That basic distinction has to be borne in mind.

6. PANEL DISCUSSION ON REGIONAL CONCERNS

This session was chaired by Shri S. K. Guha, IAS who was also the moderator for the presentations.

Mr S K Guha

We have speakers from Andhra Pradesh, Karnataka, Maharashtra, West Bengal and U.P. We will go into issues that we did not discuss in the morning, about trafficking, big money, issues of brute force, human rights abuses, etc. I would request Mr Prasad to make his presentation.

K J Prasad, (SALT, Hyderabad)

In Andhra Pradesh around 25,000 women who belong to the Domara tribe are pressed into religious prostitution. Then we have another set of women who are put into the commercial market in Mehboob Ki Mehendi in Hyderabad, Cheirala, East Godavari and West Godavari districts. We are working with 2.5 lakh women who are in this trade.

Today highway trafficking on NH-7 and NH-14 is picking up very fast through organised gangs. Each girl is paid two hundred rupees a night. These gang leaders pick them up, put them on these national highway roads and the total earnings would be collected by the gang leaders not by women.

We have organised women in 14 districts, contacted the police and the judiciary and conducted interactions with them. On 30-31 October, 1995 we had a State Convention where a state level forum was formed.

These women demand respect. They are called prostitutes, lathicharged by the police and criminalised. Is this justice? ''We are not pickpocketing, we are not looting people, we are only selling our bodies to earn our living. How are the police and dadas living? If prostitution is stopped today 50% of the police income will also be stopped. If you go to the Special Court at 8 in the morning the judge even does not investigate the charges before pronouncing his sentence and asks us to pay a penalty of Rs.50. Allow us to live and not die.'' This is what they have to say.

The fact is that we do not have Rai Sahib type of Collectors everywhere. When the Nizam of Hyderabad started the Mehboob ki Mehendi 100 years ago he made good arangements for stay, set up a hospital and a police station to protect the women. But after the establishment of the democratic Government this place has become a bazaar where women have to pay rent daily to have a place to function, where the police perpetuates all forms of extortion without providing any protection.

Sister Bridget (Karnataka)

We are working in Manvi Taluk of Karnataka in about 50 villages. In the taluk we have 700 devadasis with whom we have been associated for the last 10 years. When we first came to the village we did not know that they were devadasis. Later on we discovered that girls are dedicated to goddess Yellamma but they live a life of prostitution. These devadasis are respected in the community and not looked down upon because they are supposed to do God's work. The rich people of the village are using them for their pleasure. These girls are all from dalit background but the men who visit them are from the high caste. The interesting thing is that they are not allowing their own daughters from the upper caste to join them, only girls belonging to lower caste are being dedicated.

We began our work amongst them. In the beginning we had a lot of problems both from the devadasis and from the upper caste people of the village. Gradually we were able to visit them and talk to them. Later on when they realised that our mission was not conversion, they became friendly and we gained their confidence.

Now we have organised 700 women into groups called Mahila Sanghas. There are some devadasis who have not come to us. But most of them who are collaborating with us are actively involved with us to eradicate this devadasi system.

During the festival of Yellamma girls are dedicated to the godess. For the past four years we have been trying to make these people stop their own practice. These women have come forward to say that they would join in processions and protest on that particular day. In the first year we staged a street play in which these devadasi women themselves participated. These women had the courage to say that they were suffering devadasis and they did not want any other girl to be initiated into this system in the name of God. Now they have the courage even to ask the high caste people as to why only women from their caste be dedicated and not women from upper caste.

In Manvi Taluka where we are working there is a lot of control over this system because people in other villages also have come to know that there is an organisation that is working for devadasis. The youth from different villages are aware that this evil practice should be checked. When they come to know that there is any dedication, they inform us. When we come to know we enter the village. In the beginning police was not supporting us but now the police has understood our work and they support us. Even the tehsildar and the BDO extend their help. I must say that the Government is really helping us in this movement. In one case we had to take the Collector with us because they would not allow us to enter the village and they were determined to dedicate the girl and all the ceremonies were being performed. We took photographs of the ceremonies and the Collector visited place. As a result the brother and the father of the girl were put in jail.

The girls are not happy to be dedicated. They are forced by parents who do it because they do not have sons to earn or look after them. In this system the prostitutes remain in the house and therefore the money comes home. We are trying to get help from the Government and we have trained some of them at our tailoring certres. The problem is that the Government gives them land but the land is such that it cannot be cultivated. When they do not cultivate Government threatens to take it back. Alongwith land they should be given implements so that they can cultivate the land.

Mr. B.L. Patil (Athni, Karnataka)

My organisation Vimochana came in to existence in Karnataka becaue of the initiative taken by the JWP which took up this subject in Karnataka for the first time.

We helped in setting up of a dairy unit of 20 such devadasis, 40 in the weaving unit, 5 in nylon rope making, 20 in wool spinning and 20 in the garment unit. To admit frankly, these programmes have been a failure. This is because my sisters in the profession are incapable of hard work since their health has been completely ruined.

After five years of experience we realised that we have to target the children of these women. For the first time in the history of this nation a school has been started for the children of the devadasis in the state of Karnataka. It is unfortunate that the Government of Karnataka had rejected our proposal for 8 acres of land. A lady then came forward and donated 8 acres of land in a remote village in a taluka on the border of Maharashtra. Last year the first batch of SSC students took the exams. Out 21 children 17 got first division.

I believe that we have to change the structure and the mentality of the society. Rehabilitation projects are necessary but education of children is essential because it is they who can transform that society. For doing this I sincerely request all the voluntary institutions to make provision for free education for those children in the atmosphere of a residential school. Ours is a residential school where mothers are allowed to visit their children at any time they want.

Usha Wagh (Pune, Maharashtra)

I would begin from where Patilji stopped. There is a group of organisations in Maharashtra that works for the prostitutes. I am one of them. I would like to put forward some of my observations which are based on my own experiences.

Majority of women in prostitution are devadasis belonging to the community of dancers and singers who dedicated themselves to God. It is society which gives sanction to these women. In Maharashtra because of the better facilities for education some women have left prostitution. However, in Pune there are women in prostitution who have migrated from other places like Nepal, women who are in the profession because of poverty, or because they have been desrted by their husbands, or those who have been raped. In Pune their living conditions are better, medical health is better organised, doctors treat these women with contempt. The problems of women in prostitution in Pune are with regard to the education and future of their children.

I agree with my friends from Karnataka that there is the influence of casteism and communalism even in the system of prostitution. Dalit women are looked down upon even within prostitution. When a customer goes his first preference is for a high caste prostitute. We should try to understand that most Dalit women do not go into prostitution because of poverty or because they have been victims of rape or because of religious traditions. They are forced into prostitution because they are Dalit. We must give thought to this problem which is on the increase.

It is very important that the middle class community should be sensitised about this problem. They still look at this problem with contempt and look down upon these women and feel they do not require solution. Most of the people feel that prostitutes and children of prostiitutes have no right to live.

Child prostitutes need extra care and we are thinking of drawing up schemes for their education. But till such time I have a suggestion for the interim period. There are a number of central and state Government educational schemes for school going girls. The admission rules are strict and children of prostitues can not get admission there. They do not have their father's name nor do they have proof of residence and income. We should recommend that these girls be given special preference in admission to schools if recommended by an NGO.

Q. J. Zaidi (Allahabad, U.P.)

I am representing a city where people from all over the country go to wash away their sins. Here people of status patronise these women but refuse to give them their rightful status.

It is in these conditions that we began some work in Allahabad. There are many Dalit women in prostitution. In Allahabad, we have women from all areas. There are eleven lanes known by the areas from where these women come, Madrasi gali, Bengali gali, Marathi gali, etc. Women who come to these lanes do not live there for more than 6 months. From Allahabad they go to Kanpur, Delhi, etc. and then again come back to Allahabad after a year. As for the local prostitutes they have been subjected to harsh repression. The officer who was sitting here yesterday 4, years back forced these women to undergo AIDS test and charged them Rs. 300.

After the tests 15 women were sent to Nari Niketan. We went to meet them. Of the women tested six were declared HIV positive. Three died in hospitals and there was nobody to look after them. They were not even served food. They died within a week and were not even seen by a doctor. When we sent SOS to the Central Government we received the reply after one and a half month asking us to furnish details where they were admitted.

No recognised educational institution is ready to give admission to the children of women in prostitution. No institution is ready to give them education whether the institution is church related, public or Government. The moment their father's name is asked they are at a loss.

Today there are 518 women with whom we sit and work. Whenever they are attacked by the rescue officers we go and obtain their bail. Police repression is so much that many women have been forced to leave their places of work and move to smaller localities. They act as call girls. They come as anganwadi workers, teachers, clerks etc., do their trade and return home in the evening. There are a few women who operate at night and call themselves air hostesses, nurses etc.

We need to provide alternate jobs for these women. There is no programme run by the Government in Allahabad to rehabilitate them.

UP has become a transit point for prostitutes. I am sure that the sensitive NGOs and officials of the Governemt would come and help in the cause. I hope we can come together and fight for the rights of these women and give them their rightful place in the society.

Ajit Singh, Varanasi

We have gone through all stages of protest including a dharna in front of National Commission for Women. Isn't it strange that these women have to protest against National Commission for Women for their demands.

The society has to play an important role even before rehabilitation. Why is society silent about police brutality? If you are silent you are ratifying the action. I began by adopting three such children. I had a very bitter experience. The whole exercise backfired. Do you think you will be able to rehabilitate them when the society is not ready to accept them?

I would like to say that when we talk about coercion we begin to talk about the pimps. It is important to include police and society also in that category.

Police is pimp of the pimps. If the police does not support the system no girl can ever come to this trade. Everyone knows that there is a fixed amount of Rs. 20,000 on each girl who is traded. If the girls do not come the income of the police would also end. The girls come from Nepal or to the same red light areas and if they are intercepted at that stage there is no reason why this system will continue.

How does one fight the police? We do not have the machinery to fight the police. If you have to check the pimps you can take the help of the police who can frame charges against them and catch them. My emphasis is therefore on the police. It is they who play the most important role in the link. I firmly believe that once we have given them a lead we should step aside and let them play their role. If they can take up the fight themselves we would have achieved a very important landmark. Pimps work in collusion with the police. If you can get the police on your side, the pimps will become weaker. This would be the first step towards rehabilitation. The question of vocational training comes after these pimps and police are checked. Unless these women are free vocational training has no meaning.

What collector D.S. Rai has said is very positive. The tragedy is that all of us are neither IAS nor do we have his kind of people everywhere. What comes to our mind we cannot implement because we are not IAS. It is my bad experience that from policeman to DC everyone speaks the same language.

Subir Banerjee (Calcutta)

I am representing the 'Shelter for Homeless'. We are working in Calcutta and surrounding areas. We are running a school in Sonagachi. This school is has been operational since 1991 and has children aged 3 to 14 years. At first we faced a lot of obstacles in entering the area. Subsequently we were accepted. The red light area women were always apprehensive of anyone coming to their area. With time they have realised that we were genuine social workers.

Among the children of these women there are some meritorious students. From time to time we have organised recreational programmes for cultural exposure of these children. We got a very good response.

We have tried to provide some vocational training to the boys, in motor mechanics, etc. We have also Mahila Mandal for prostitutes in Howrah, in Khiderpur and Metiabruz.

Lalitha, S. A., (Joint Women's Programe, Delhi)

In this meeting there are women who belong to the red light area where I am working and I asked if they would like to narrate any of their experiences but they have asked me to speak on their behalf.

On behalf of the Joint Women's Programme we began our work in 1988 at the GB Road, near Ajmeri Gate. A voluntary doctor and myself first went there to learn about their experience. When I visited them for the first time I realised that what we read in the newspaper was all wrong. If there is any respect for humanity in Delhi it is only in the red light area of Delhi. We were welcomed and they spoke to us freely. We did not face any problem in our work right from the first day.

We started to visit them with some medicines and doctors. Then we started taking them to doctors who were sympathetic to the cause. Later they asked us to open a centre for their children. After talking to the Welfare Department of the Government, the Joint Women's Programme started a centre. It started with five children, at present there are 68 children. We faced a lot of problems in running this centre from people other than the pimps and these women. We were able to build a rapport with women and pimps from 1988 onwards.

In 1990 there was a raid in which Mr. Amod Kanth, who was DCP, claimed to have taken away 112 children. Of 112 children 88 were women who were above the age of 20. There were women who were 40 years also who were taken in as children.

Their protest was very strong and they also indulged in road blocking and violence and they proved that their children are not neglected as was being proved under "neglected children" by JJ Act. Children who were in boarding submitted their certificates and JJ Board released those children. Police initiated a case against the JJ Board's decision and all these girls had to report to the police every Saturday. This was like a mela where people would throng to have a glimpse of the girls. An activist lawyer Shobha Agarwal got an affidavit from all these girls and fought their case for exemption. This took her one year. The case which was decided recently after five years went in favour of JJ Board's decision that they did the right thing to exempt these girls. Officers who claim that they are only following the Supreme Court decision are therefore wrong in their claims. The Joint Women's Programme was one of the many organisation that had raised its voice all over the country against this police action.

In 1989 there was the AIDS Prevention Bill and these women were being targeted for testing. We protested against their action and we had sent recommendations in collaboration with other organisations.

We cannot eradicate the prostitution system but we also do not have alternatives to offer women who would like to come out of prostitution. They have shelter at GB Road. They can earn a living to sustain themselves but if they leave that place where would they go? Live on the streets? In 1990 they asked the Government to give them a job with minimum Rs.1500 salary with shelter. If that was done they were ready to leave their profession. They had put this demand when they attended the meeting with the Central Social Welfare Board Committee.

We think that they are entitled to the basic amenities which is their right. They require water and ration. They should get I Card but there are organisations and Government also who are putting obstacles in that.

Our Day Care Centre is run in a verandah of the MCD School and we are trying hard with the Education Department to give us another room but we have not been successful so far. The girls are ready to break open that room but we restrain them from doing so. We are trying to provide them basic facilities.

We are trying to get them I Cards and some women were photographed. We are not claiming that we are working in the whole of GB Road. There are approximately3,500 dancing girls and women in prostitution in that area. We are in touch with about 2,500 women. We not only talk to them about AIDS but also about other diseases.

We tell them about the neccessity of condoms in prevention of AIDS and other diseases but these women are asking for better quality condoms. We have been asking the National AIDS Control Organisation to provide for better quality condoms since they have the funds from the Government and World Bank. They prefer to return the money rather than distributing condoms for a cause. We however get good quality deluxe condoms from the wholesale market and sell them to these women at the same price. We also collect them from LNJP Hospital which are available under the Family Planning scheme and distribute them free to these women. Earlier these women used to go and get it from the hospital but now we have to go to pick them up. Unless we go Nirodh boxes do not reach us at the centre.

These are the problems local women there are facing. We are trying to do something with many of the organisations that are working there. At times work goes on smoothly, at times there are differences of opinion. We have set up a women's organisation called Mashal Mahila Sanghathan. Then there is a Mashal Shiksha Kendra, which is run under JWP guidance.

Ms. Leela (G B Road, Delhi)

Our children go the Mashal Shiksha Kendra for education. Elder children go to the hostel. The Police creates a lot of problem for us. Everyday they pick up one or two girls and lock them up or just threaten them for bribes. We live under constant fear and the SHO is not the man whom we can look up for protection. He even does not care to find out what are the charges under which our sisters are being framed or arrested. They ask for a bribe and if we do not pay they put us behind bars. This is repeated everyday.

If you are serious about doing something for us we request you to do something to stop this police brutality.

Leo Monteiro (Manipur)

The system of prostitution in Manipur or in the Northeast is quite different from that of the other states that I have been hearing since yesterday. In Manipur and Assam there are army informers who are actually pimps and they supply girls to the police and the army.

You must have heard about the combing operations and the raids conducted on the Naga villages and in Assam. There are so many cases of rape, sexual assault and abuses during these operations. Nothing is reported. Prostitution can be seen in border areas connecting India and Burma. Also in Guwahati which is the communication centre for the NorthEast there is some prostitution Poverty, tradition, cultural practices have generally not driven many girls into prostitution.

In these areas drug trade is carried on by the women folk. They hide the drugs in the vagina to cross the borders. Whoever is a drug peddler is expected to be a prostitute. If these women are caught they are raped in the prison even if they are not prostitutes.

Y.K. Gautam, (Bihar)

I represent Jan Jagaran Sansthan, Nalanda. In Bihar there are four major towns Muzaffarpur, Mungher, Purnea & Gaya which are known for their red light areas. In Muzaffarpur the red light area is known as Chhaturbhuj; in Purnea the place is known as Gulab; in Gaya it known as Chowk Road and in Mungher it is known as Sarvan Bazaar.

There are two or three types of prostitution in our area. One is traditional, second is forced prostitution where prostitutes have been purchased in the market. In the third category are Dalit women who have to do this for living. Most of them are in it because they have either been deserted by their husbands or are widows and hence are forced by circumstances to join prostitution.

In these areas no one is concerned about the problem of the other brothel next door. Everyone is busy in her own work. However if there is any communal harmony it is in these red light areas. You can get women from different religions in the same brothel. The dholak player may be a Muslim, dancer may be a Hindu.

In Gaya we have started the work in the field of education for children. Balwadi programmes are being run. Then there are programmes relating to AIDS awareness and there is also an AIDS counselling centre in the red light area. This programme is designed in the interest of both the prostitutes and the customers. The results have been good.

Last month a team under Dr. T.K. Jaina, Senior Research Officer, from AIIMS visited this area to monitor the work in this field. Rasya, a prostitute was asked about her reaction to this programme. She asked the team person to remove the bedsheet and showed them a packet of condom. This was the biggest achievement of this programme. It is a must for any customer to use the condoms. If all prostitutes speak one language the customer would have no choice. We are in touch with the health centres and they have also co-operated in distributing condoms. The administration is extending all help in this programme.

As for their interaction with the police we have been organising regular meetings of the administration, police and the prostitutes and we have also have made arrangements for free legal aid. Earlier we had to look for advocates but ever since the police has started to co-operate there is no need for advocates. The local police is not harassing the prostitutes.

The movement for eradication of prostitution can only be successful if not only prostitutes but also the men who are attached to this trade are rehabilitated. If you try to take an action by force you cannot succeed. Now we have started a programme to involve them in the making of Agarbatis which are famous in Gaya.

If we start Credit and Thrift Societies in the red light areas, with small amounts, in course of time there would be good capital. We can only give them technical support. Their money will be deposited in their own area and they would govern that money through their representatives. The small group may have only 5 persons. Big group would be of 40 women. Any woman who wants to take a loan can get it within half an hour. Whether interest has to be charged would be decided by that co-opeative. We have suggested that the interest should not be charged if the loan is for 15 days.

We feel that there should be a national network of NGOs and every year we should meet at different places.

Raphael Paulson (Kerala)

We started a very small pogramme a few months back in Calicut. Our success is that we are still working there and have not been thrown out. Our fight is against exploitation and discrimination of women in the name of prostitution.

We have been discussing about the rehabilition programmes throughout the day. First of all we were all blaming the police for the atrocities being committed. I am not denying that police is not committing atrocities in fact we are also facing a lot of problems with the police. But when we talk about rehabilitation most of the time it is because we think that they are involved in immoral, anti social thing. We feel it is our responsibility to bring them out of that. I think it was not included in the plan but in course of time we realised that rehabilitation is necessary. I think it should come as a gradual consequence of our intervention. I say this because simply taking a woman out of her profession and trying to rehabillitate her in society is not going to work at all. We all know it.

The place I am working is called Bangladesh colony. This colony has major concentration of women in prostitution and all other anti social elements also live there. Women prefer this area because there is no stigmatisation and they can move about freely. The brothel set up is not like that of Bombay or Delhi. Women live there and go to the cities pick up their clients take them to lodges, carry on their business and come back to their place. In this place they can move about the share their feelings with others, without stigmatisation or harassment. There is exploitation but compared to civilised areas they are more comfortable here.

One important point is the element of drug addiction. It is not only a health problem, it is a legal problem. For the police it is easy. They pick up women from this community and charge them whenever they need cases.

Mr. S K Guha

We have had a very good discussion starting from Andhra Pradesh, Karnataka, Bihar, Uttar Pradesh, Bengal, Delhi, Maharashtra, Manipur, Madhya Pradesh and Kerala. Many issues have been raised.

1. Mr Prasad spoke of human rights aspects of prostitutes. He spoke of self respect and self esteem. He elaborated at length about police brutality and bias. He spoke on the need for organising and mobilising them. He hinted at the larger issue of trafficking taking on dangerous dimensions and the big money involved.

2. In Karnataka, Sister Bridget spoke of the devadasis. She raised the important point of there being a caste element in this whole practice where Dalits were devadasis and upper castes were customers. She too spoke of the need for mobilising and organising them.

3. We had Mr. Patil from Karnataka mostly speaking of the devadasis but he raised the basic point whether economic rehabilitation is really possible on a sustainable basis. Very often these women are physically impaired because of their lifestyles and the suffering they have gone through, and therefore possibly there is a need to focus on children of prostitutes so that we can break this inter generational cycle of prostitution.

4. From Maharashtra, Usha spoke of the need to focus on children and the need to involve prostitutes in any meaningful programmes of rehabilitation or welfare. She also spoke at length on the aspect of caste. How prostitution is a manifestation of caste system which pushes Dalit

women into the prostitution. She spoke of the education system and how rules have to be relaxed if interventions in education need to be made. She said that till they had new schemes existing schemes will have to be converted on to them and the schemes will have to be converged on to them and the schemes will have to be the special focus towards this category of children of prostitutes.

5. From UP, Mr. Zaidi spoke of the exploitative nature of the system and how it makes the Dalit women the victims. He also spoke of prostitution in big cities like Allahabad where there is a lot of mobility and migration. He also spoke of police torture, Government indifference, and difficulties in having to run the programme for them and even getting accommodation for running these programmes.

6. Ajit spoke largely about the struggle with police and the Government and bureaucracy. He also spoke of the National Commission for Women and about the frustrating experience he had. But he was saying that a start has to be made and we have to target the police and the administration through better sensitisation. NGOs could be used to do this sensitisation and creating a forum in which this effort could be carried out on a sustainable basis.

7. From West Bengal Mr. Bannerjee talked about the efforts of that his organisation in Sonagachi. How the breaking of initial distrust is so important when you go into these red light areas there is distrust which you have to break. He spoke of the need for vocational training.

8. From Delhi Lalitha spoke of GB Road. She raised the basic question of the concept of neglected juvenile. She referred to the Juvenile Justice Act wherein any child found in the red light area was presumed to be neglected and therefore the state had the right to remove that child from that area. In fact the ITPA also has similar presumptions : that any child found in the red light area would

mean that the child had been kept there for the purpose of prostitution. This is an important aspect. The ITPA is going through review for the purpose of amendment and suggestions have been made by the National Law School whom we had engaged for study. She also spoke of the need for providing basic amenities in these areas. She raised the issue of identity cards.

9. From GB Road we heard Leela who spoke of police torture and what was clear was that there was a felt need among them to send their children to schools, to give them good education. In fact one of the studies has shown that the education level of children of prostitute was higher than that of other children in similar areas. The lesson is that the system must come up with responses to meet this felt need for education among these groups for education of their children.

10. Mr. Leo spoke of the insurgency situation in Manipur, which has created a different kind of problem with the army being the biggest customer. He spoke of how sexual assault during combing operations creates these situations and leads to prostitution.

11. From Bihar, Mr. Gautam said that there was very little interaction between the inmates of the red light areas. I think the moral is that mobilisation and organisation is possibly is the first step if we have to achieve anything meaningful. He spoke of the programmes for the children of prostitutes, the education programmes and so on. But he made an interesting point that Government programmes should not be such as to create dependency. He gave this example of Thrift and Credit societies. The formation of thrift groups would be an interesting intervention and there are mechanisms such as Mahila Kosh.

I think we ran through the whole gamut of issues and the house is now open for discussion.

DISCUSSION

Rita Panicker, Butterflies, (New Delhi)

We work with street children. The biggest frustration that we face is that the judicial system is so slow in getting the case completed that it is very frustrating for the child and for us. There should be speeding up of the judicial system specially with the juvenile justice system.

The National Human Rights Commission very recently published a statement in which they said that you have to humanise the police force. I think that is important because we witness the police brutality practically everyday, the way they beat up our children and also our activists whenever they have tried to intervene. They were arrested on the charges that they were obstructing the policeman from performing their duty –at that point of time they were beating the children! I personally think that we should mobilise public opinion against police brutality, corruption and ignorance of the law.

The other point is about the whole area of sex tourism. As you know India is promoting tourism and there are certain areas in our country which are now becoming famous for sex tourism. I hope this country doesn't become like Philippines, Sri Lanka and Thailand. It is important that for paedophiles who have been caught red handed their photographs, their nationalities and passport numbers are notified to the concerned authorities so that they become persona grata and are never given visas to enter this country. I would also recommend that this information should be shared within the SAARC region so that they do not travel to Sri Lanka, Nepal and Bangladesh as well and to other Asian countries like Thailand and Philippines, and to Russia where sex tourism is on the increase.

Usha Wagh, Pune, Maharashtra

Dalit women as a group are always susceptible to prostitution because they are often raped by the high caste or influential men. Hence they are likely to fall into prostitution. That is why more Dalit women are found in prostitution.

The liquor business also has a connection with prostitution. There was a case in Maharashtra where hotels and bars had young girls serving liquor. The effect of that is that it converts them to prostitution making them open to exploitation by the monied people. You may have read in the papers that 200 girls were the victims of such prostitution. There were letters to Maharashtra Government and our Minister concerned with this department argued that since they could not provide the alternative jobs for these girls, they were not going to deprive them by closing the bars.

K J Prasad, Hyderabad

The cultural tradition is that the lower strata women are the slaves and the higher strata the exploitators. At the time of marriage the Dalit woman goes to the house of the landlords and serves the guests and the landlords. However, she is not allowed to give birth to his child. Always her pregnancy is terminated. Today in A.P. itself more than 20000 women in prostitution are coming from the Scheduled Castes and Scheduled Tribes.

Jyotsna Chatterji, JWP

Some years' ago we had made a study on trafficking of girls for sexual exploitation. We found that of the 100 cases that had been interviewed 58 were from Scheduled Castes and Scheduled Tribes background. In fact I was tempted to call that bit of research "caste in prostitution". That material is still with us and I cannot understand why in a country where caste is such an important factor, where all power is in the hands of a particular section of society, it is natural that a woman who is discriminated is a Dalit. So prostitution of women belonging to the Scheduled Castes is natural because that is the group that is going to be discriminated against always. That is what Ushaji is trying to say that most of the women in prostitution come from the Scheduled Castes and Tribes background. There is a lot of research and study to prove that.

Lalitha S.A., JWP, Delhi

When you say that under the JJ Act or under the Immoral Traffic Prevention Act the police have a right to pick up children who are in the red light area, but there are no alternate places to keep their 5 or 6 year old children. I think the law has to change. Mothers are not keeping their children there by wish but by compulsion. By forcibly isolating these children we create a new group in the society. The women in prostitution themselves understand the problem and they do not want there children to live in the brothel. I am only telling you the practical problem. We are not able to run our centre at night to keep away the children from their mothers because we do not have the space. We have been working and running round and yet we have not been able to get extra space. It is very difficult to make the bureaucracy work, by the time you motivate one official he is transferred. How can organisations work like this? We are accountable to these women for whom we are fighting. They ask us why is there so much injustice?

There should be a method to convince people without using force. If you convince them that children should not live where the mothers carry on the trade they may relent. It is wrong to forcibly pick up children and announce in the press that the Government has adopted all children of the prostitutes. Is it right to call them prostitutes? That is her trade and profession which you have to recognise. They are women in prostitution and we have no right to call them prostitutes. We have to change our attitude and mindset.

K J Prasad, SALT, Hyderabad

I would like to make recommendation for passing a resolution regarding these identity cards. We are facing the same problem in Andhra Pradesh. All these women in prostitution have been eliminated in the election lists. So we have written letters to the State Election Commission giving the numbers and locations requesting them to appoint a special team to go into the areas and take their identities. But till date there is no response.

Mr. S K Guha

They were not in the voters list earlier. But the Chief Election Commissioner has directed precisely that this time they should be included and given identity cards. The electoral registration officers responsible have all got that circular. I think organisations should meet these EROs who are sub-divisional magistrates and see to it that it is implemented.

K J Prasad, Hyderabad

The problem with them is that for the past one year they have been trying to get a ration card. The authorities say that you come with the voters' identity card and we will give you the ration card. Now when we go for voter's identity card the name is not there in the rolls.

Lalitha S.A. JWP, Delhi

We are raising the issue of identity card here because if you issue the Idenity card to all women of the area when anyone applies afresh you would know who are the new girls and women who have come into the profession. This could be one way to keep track of new entrants.

Gautam, JWP, Delhi.

These women have a lot of problem about ration cards. Most of the women do not possess a ration card. Those who are very old residents may possess a ration card but the new women do not have a ration card. If they try through a middle man they charge them Rs. 500.

D S Rai, M.P.

I want to take the opportunity of putting forth some observations and place them before the representatives of many organisations who are present here.

Most of the development and welfare plans have 40% reservation for women whether it is under IRDP or any plan. The local officers like Block Development Officer and others are unable to implement these reservations. We must see that these schemes are implemented.

During the discussion we had asked several sisters who are present here to present their views but they were hesitant to express themselves. I should have brought some of the sisters from my area. These women who have now left prostitution have the confidence to address a 1000 strong audience. Unless the quality of leadership is not developed among these women we will not be able to wean the women from prostitution.

S K Guha

Presently all the states have set up state level committees to look into the issue of child prostitution, except the states of Bihar, Pondicherry and J & K. I know that this will not do any magic but it is one of the ways.

During this discussion very important issues have come up relating to legislation change, attitudinal change, creating economic options and basic issues of caste and communalism which we tend to push under the carpet. All of you have contributed to this and personally it has been a learning experience for me. I am sure this discussion could lead to important resolutions which could influence decision making. I hope that based on these deliberations we can actually derive intervention particularly in the field of children.

Jyotsna Chatterji

On behalf of the participants and the JWP I thank Mr Guha for helping us with the deliberations and chairing this session.

If you look around the table you will see that 50% of the brothers and sisters are representing JWP related groups. These JWP related groups have been delibertely and consciously created for networking. Today we hope that we are able to form a coalition with other groups present here on the issue of women in prostitution, so that we can effectively do the work towards prevention, rehabilitation and lobbying with the Government.

7.

HUMAN RIGHTS PERSPECTIVES AND PLAN OF ACTION

Chairperson: Ms Jyotsna Chatterji :

The title of our workshop was "Women in Prostitution - Human Rights Perspectives". During our presentations we had kept in mind the fact that it is essential for us to remember that women in prostitution are human beings like us and are citizens of this country having equal rights.

People present here know that one of the objectives of the workshop was to build a closer network among organisations that are working with prostitutes, their children and children in prostitution.

We have with us here as speaker for the day Ms. Ann-Lis Svensson, Deputy Director of UNICEF. I would like to invite her to share her views with us and lead us further in our deliberations.

Ms Ann-Lis Svensson, Deputy Director, UNICEF

The girl child is born with all the potential powers that any child has. During childhood this is taken away from most of them and that is why we need programmes for empowerment of women.

Child prostitution is child rape. All of us gathered here are horrified by this evil and that is why we are here. We all know that systematic trafficking of girls for profit by experienced individuals account for the greatest number of girls transported and sold in India. Their lives are treated as commodities in the market. These are children who have been betrayed and stigmatised for life, children to whom the society and Government is deeply in debt for not having protected them. They can never be compensated or rehabilitated. The Beijing Platform for Action stipulates that medical, social and psychological support services must be provided to assist girls who are subjected to such violence. This must be done but we all agree it is far more important to prevent this abuse. I think we need to write a chapter on programme of action on prevention.

The powerful are allowed to continue their business and children continue to be victimised. The time has come to disarm the protection extended to the powerful exploiters. Instead we should form a strong alliance around the vulnerable and see that they are the ones who are protected and not the exploiters.

There must be a change in the power balance, a strengthened democracy that respects all groups in the society. India is fortunate to have the world's finest human rights document as the basis of its governance and national conduct. I refer to the Constitution of India. India also belongs to SAARC, the first inter-country group to declare the decade for the girl child. Let the Constitution of India, the SAARC Declaration, the Convention on the Rights of the Child, and the Convention on the Elimination of all Forms of Discrimination Against Women become instruments of liberation for the most vulnerable among the vulnerable.

The Convention on the Rights of the Child which is the Magna Carta of Child Rights was adopted unanimously by the UN General Assembly in 1989. It is a major step forward to expand the world's legal boundaries, embracing and legitimising the needs of children and providing the legal and moral basis of their survival, development and protection. In the short span of six years it has become one of the most widely accepted human rights document in history. By ratifying it, more than

135 Governments have committed themselves to take measures to prevent and protect children from "unlawful and sexual practices and exploitative use in prostitution, pornography and from abduction, sale and trafficking".

India is a country where 4 million girls are missing. Much has been said about the systematic deprivation and unequal treatment of girls. Very little is known about the discrimination and deprivation faced by children who are sexually abused and sold in the sex trade.

We have observed that to a large extent the causes of the problem of child prostitution are similar to the causes of child labour. Some of them are exploitation of the weak and the underprivileged; economic, social and gender related discrimination and exploitation. As a result of this these families have not got access to the services as provided. One service which is very important is education. Education seldom reaches these families.

While talking about rehabilitation, you need to keep in mind the needs of the child. If you provide the services after the harm has been done you will try to compensate the harm but you do not always get to the root of the problem. You must ensure that they become part of the education and health system.

May I venture to suggest that this coming together of so many concerned people could become an occasion for launching of a national network with anyone of the organisation present here volunteering to be a national secretariat and perhaps making a protection action network against child abuse.

DISCUSSION

Q J Zaidi, Allahabad

The figures you are quoting are not true. This is because a large number of cases in the villages are never reported. This is just a national figure of children in prostitution.

Ann-Lis Svensson

I would agree with that. It is not a question of the numbers, but the number of missing children refers to the low status of girl child.

Vijay Thakur, Hyderabad

In India we have not only inter-state migration but also inter-country. The Himalayan kingdom of Nepal is one place from where girls are trafficked into India This means that international policing is a very big factor. The international policing though highly equipped to control narcotic trafficking, has made a very little dent in the last ten years in the area of trafficking in women. We really need to pin down international policing agencies and critique their role.

Ann-Lis Sevssson

I do not think that the Government alone can solve all problems. It requires a strong social movement to demand justice delivery.

Sr. Shalini S.C.N., Indian Social Institute, New Delhi.

You made a comment that UNICEF is planning a consultation of interest groups. May I make a very strong recommendation to the UNICEF that when you do invite these interest groups you do consider who you are inviting. The people you invite must be from grassroots level and you must not limit it to elite NGOs who speak English. Only when the UN recognises such grassroot bodies will there be a shift in the power balance.

Shyamala Nataraj (Madras)

We have been discussing the human rights of women in prostitution and of children in prostitution. My concern is that all us who are sitting here think alike about the problem. However there are a number of people who are thinking about this problem with a very different perspective and who are able to exert the right pressure to get policy changes. But the question of making large changes especially when we are talking human rights has to do with large segments of people and with public attitudes as well. It is one area that we have not talked about in the last two days.

Y K Gautam, Bihar

We should concentrate on making the national network and of apportioning the responsibility to an organisation. I would suggest that any organisation taking up this responsiblity should be based in Delhi which can be approached by other organisations from the rest of the country. Since Joint Women's Programme has been involved in this issue for the past so many years we would urge them to take up this responsibility.

D. S. Rai

I would like to expand on what Shyamala was saying. She was right in a way. We like minded people have decided on one course of action but a very wide section of the population does not think on those lines. She was right when she said that a common course of action should be decided upon and followed.

8.
RESOLUTIONS PASSED AT THE WORKSHOP ON WOMEN IN PROSTITUION : HUMAN RIGHTS PERSPECTIVES

TRAFFICKING IN WOMEN AND CHILDREN FOR PROSTITUTION

1. The govt. should strictly enforce the laws regarding trafficking and the help of voluntary organisations should be enlisted in this regard if the nexus among police, pimps and politicians is to be broken.

2. Efforts should be made to identify those areas that may fall prey to traffickers and vigilance must be stepped up in these areas so as to prevent young and minor girls from falling into the hands of the pimps.

3. The national police should work in close co-operation with the INTERPOL in detecting international traffic which originates at national levels and operates through local agents.

4. As poverty is one of the primary reasons for trafficking in girls and women the govt. should seriously implement its poverty alleviation programmes.

5. The government should implement the U.N. Convention on Elimination of all Forms of Discrimination Against Women (CEDAW) and The Convention on the Rights of the Child.

6. The government should enact a comprehensive legilsation to curb the growing menance of sex tourism and trans border trafficking.

7. Sensitizing of the community to act as watchdog is necessary in order to prevent entry of children into prostitution and to identify and inform police about traffickers and take follow up action.

LAW

FOR WOMEN

1. We are against the legalisation of prostituion in the Indian context, where women and children are forced into the profession due to poverty and other causes and thereafter remain in the clutches of pimps for the rest of their life.

2. That the ITPA Act be amended - Changes have to be made in s.7(i) and 8(b) that prohibit prostitution in public places. These sections criminalise the prostitute, forcing her to live in inhuman conditions in so-called red light areas.

3. We also demand enhanced punishment for the customers who are the primary culprits and who create a market for the exploitation of women in the form of prostitution.

4. Section 20 of the ITPA also requires change. Under this the magistrate is given discretionary powers to ask a sex worker to vacate her premises if there is a complaint against her. This provision is almost always used as a tool to harrass the woman. We demand removal of this discretionary power.

5. We demand compulsory registration of marriages.

6. We urge parents not to get their daughters married to strangers without verifying their bona fides.

7. Legal education should be systematically given, covering the laws and their implementation to all women and the police personnel and other functionaries.

FOR CHILDREN

8. We demand a humanised treatment of children of prostitutes in Juvenile Homes.

9. We demand the setting up of effective advisory bodies consisting of NGO representatives to monitor the functioning of these homes.

10. The Juvenile Justice Act should also be modified so that children of prostitues are not harrassed by the police in the name of rehabilitation.

11. Foreign tourists who are child molesters and paedophiles, when identified, the Ministry of External Affairs and immigration officials should be notified and these men should be declared persona non grata.

12. We should also share the information among the SAARC countries Thailand, Philippines, Burma, Cambodia and Russia.

13. We must appeal to European and North American countries that have not passed a law, to punish such men under their national laws and also help prevent trafficking of women and girls.

HEALTH :

FOR WOMEN & CHILDREN

1. We demand primary and reproductive health care for sex workers. They should have access to both govt. and private registered medical practitioners in order to save them from quacks.

2. We demand free availabity of condoms to every sex worker, in order to save them from unwanted pregnancies and STDs.

3. We demand accountability of govt. doctors under the Consumer Protection Act.

4. No law should be used for conducting forcible HIV/AIDS tests.

REHABILITATION :

FOR WOMEN

1. The voluntary welfare organisations should receive adequate support and cooperation from the police and other govt. departments in order to help:

   a) women and girls in danger of falling into prostitution,

   b) those women and girls who are already trapped in brothels,

   c) aged sex workers who cannot earn a living, and,

   d) those suffering from AIDS.

2. The orientation of rehabilitation must be changed from one that is corrective to one that perceives women and children in prostitution as human beings who are the victims and survivors of an exploitative system.

3. We demand setting up of a data bank regarding prostitution and trafficking for that would enable us to decide on a future course of action.

4. Women in prostitution need to be mobilised and leadership qualities instilled in them in order to enable them to be their own advocates.

5. Gender sensitisation of the law and order machinery.

6. Sensitisation of menfolk of communities where women are traditionally involved in prostitution.

7. It is resolved to ensure that women in red light areas have a right to possess ration cards and voters identity cards. Official circulars should be released to all magistrates, state election commissioners for ensuring the entry of these women in the voters lists.

8. Establishment of night shelters in public places, close to police booths to help homeless, run away girls.

9. More short stay homes, which are well looked after, be provided.

FOR CHILDREN

10. Free and compulsory education for children of prostitutes in mainstream schools.

11. We strongly protest discrimination of any kind in educational institutions.

12. A National Child Rights Commission must be established so that children and adults on behalf of children can file complaints regarding violations of their rights especially with regard to sexual abuse, trafficking and children forced into prostitution. NGOs must be a part of this Commission that should be given more teeth than the NCW and the NHRC so as to take direct action against the offenders.

13. A media monitor consisting of media personnel who are concerned and committed to the cause of children should be set up. Concerned NGOs should also be part of it. This media monitor should, on a regular basis publish in the newspapers, acts of ommission and commission by the govt. in the interests of children who have fallen or may fall into prostitution and sexual abuse.

14. Strict action must be taken to eradicate child prostitution.

The workshop concluded with the setting up of a **National Networking Committee** with Joint Women's Programme as the Convenor. The address of this committee would be 14 Jangpura B, Mathura Road, New Delhi - 110014.

The workshop also demanded that a Central Statutory Body be set up similar to the Narocotics Control Bureau for the following purposes :

i) Monitor enforcement of the laws : Juvenile Justice Act, IPTA, IPC, and Cr. P.C.

ii) Monitor & Advise rehabilitation programmes.

iii) Take preventive action

iv) Establish a Data Bank

Similar bodies be set up in each state to interact, monitor and control any action related to the above in collaboration with the Central Body.

ANNEXURE

LIST OF CHAIRPERSONS

MS. MOHINI GIRI
Chairperson
National Commission for Women
Deen Dayal Upadhyay Marg
New Delhi - 110 002

Ms. JYOTSNA CHATTERJI
Director
Joint Women's Programme
14 Jangpura B
New Delhi - 110 014

PROF. LOTIKA SARKAR
L 1/ 10 , Haus Khas
New Delhi - 110 016

DR. MEERA SHIVA
c/o V. H. A. I.
Tong Swasthya Bhawam
40 InstitutionalArea
New Delhi - 110 016

MS. PADMA SETH
13 Mahavir Road
New Delhi - 110 001

MS. SARLA GOPALAN
Secretary
Department of Women and Child
Shastri Bhavan, A-Wing
New Delhi

MR. S. K. GUHA (IAS)
M-2787, Netaji Nagar
New Delhi

RESOURCE PERSONS

SHRI D.S. RAI
Collector
District Raisen
Madhya Pradesh

MR. GERRY PINTO
UNICEF
India Country Office
73, Lodhi Estate
New Delhi - 110 003

MS. ANN-LIS SVENSSON
Deputy Director - UNICEF
India Country Office
73, Lodhi Estate
New Delhi - 110 003

DR. PUNIT BEDI
D-49, Hauz Khas
New Delhi - 110 016

MS. VED KUMARI
G - 3 / 47, MODEL TOWN
New Delhi- 110 009

MS. JEAN D' CUNHA
402 GardenView
sector - 16A, Vashi
New Bombay - 400 703

MR. AMOD KANTH
DI /139 Satya Marg
Chanakyapuri
New Delhi - 110 021

DR. K. K. MUKHERJEE
Gram Niyojan Kendra
R - 10 /.118, New Rajnagar
Ghaziabad - 201002 (U.P.)

MS. RATNA KAPOOR
B-12, Maharani Bagh
New Delhi - 110 065

PARTICIPANTS (Out Station)

Ms. Usha Wagh
Samajwadi Janparished
861/1 Sadashiv Peth
Pune -411030

Ms. Mala
Dalit Mahila Sangathan
Pune (Maharashtra)

Mr. Leo Monteiro
Raphei Valley
Mantripukhri
Imphal-795002 (Manipur)

Rev. Q.J. Zaidi
SOUP
47B/2, C.Y. Chintamani Road
George Town
Allahabad - 211 002 (U.P.)

Ms. Grace L. Zaidi
Joint Women's Programme
47B/2, C.Y. Chintamani Road
George Town
Allahabad-211002 (U.P.)

Ms. Sumitra Devi
17/9, Swaraj Nagar
Allahabad-211002 (U.P.)

Ms. Janaki Devi
257, Katra
Allahabad - 211 002 (U.P.)

Ms. Ajit Singh
Guria
S-8/395,Khajuri Colony
Varanasi-221002
U.P.

Sr. Bridget
Good Shepherd Sisters
Daya Nivas
Manvi - 583123
Raichur Distt., Karnataka.

Sr. Jacqueline
Good Shepherd Sisters
Daya Nivas
Manvi - 583123
Raichur Distt. (Karnataka).

Ms. Purnima Sarkar
Institute for Development Education and Action
30/3A, N.S. Dutta Road
Howrah - 1

Mr. A. Chakraborty
Institute for Development Education and Action
30/3A, N.S. Dutta Road
Howrah - 1

Mr. S. Banerjee
Shelter for Homeless
National Forum of India
14/2 Sudder Street
Calcutta - 700 016

Mr. S. De
Shelter for Homeless
National Forum of India
14/2 Sudder Street
Calcutta - 700 016

Ms. Pratiba Sahay
Prakriti Women's Resource Centre
Nagpur Water Tank Road
Nagpur

Ms. Smriti Basu
Prakriti Women's Resource Centre
Nagpur Water Tank Road
Nagpur

Mr. Paulson Raphael
No.102, MES Hostel
Bank Road, Kozhikode
Kerala - 673001.

Mr. B.L. Patil
Vimochana Devadasi Punaravati Sangh
Athani, Belagaum Distt.
Karnataka - 591304.

Ms. Bharati
Vimochana Devadasi Punaravati Sangh
Athani, Belagaum Distt.
Karnataka - 591304.

Mr. Yogendra Kumar Gautam
Secretary, Jan Jaagran Sansthan
Kaghzi Mohalla, Bihar Sharif
Nalanda (Bihar) - 803 101.

Ms HemaPattanshetty
'Hoomane' Vidyagiri
Dharwad - 580 004 (Karnataka)

Dr. Siddharth Pattanshetty
Professor
Karnataka College
Dharwad - 580 001 (Karnataka)

Mr. K. J. Prasad
SALT
1-2-274/4 Srinivasanilayam
Domalguda, Hyderabad - 29

R.K.Padma
Joint Women's Programme
Hyderabad, A.P.

Mr. Rajesh Kumar
ODYSSEY, Sasaram (Bihar)
Navarang Colony
Fazalganj Sasaram, Bihar

Ms. Shobha Sakharwade
Prakriti Resource Centre For
Women And Development

Water Tank Road
Lonara, Koradi Road
NAGPUR

Mr. Ajit Singh
GURIA
S-8/395, Khajuri Colony
Varanasi - 221 002 (U.P.)

Ms. Vijaya Lakshmi
A.P. Ganika Mahila Sangham
1-2-274/1, Domalguda
Hyderabad - 29

Mr. Kalindi Rai
Social Worker
B-39, Sachiv Colony
Lohia Nagar
Patna - 20, (Bihar)

Dr. V. Thakur
INTERAIDE
Flat 201, Unique Appartments
Hyderabad - 16

Mr. M. Kumar
Friends of People
N.N.G. Road, Belpara
Madhupur
Dist. Deoghar (Bihar)

Mr. R.K.P. Singh
Jan Jagran Sanstha
Mohala Kazi
Bihar Shrief, Nalanda
Bihar

Ms. Shyamla Nataraj
South India AIDS Action Programme
65, Kamaraj Avenue, 1st Street
Adyar
Madras - 20

LOCAL PARTICIPANTS

Ms. Kailash Pati
Member
National Commission for Women
Deendayal Upadhyaya Marg
New Delhi - 110 002

Ms. Ganga Potai
Member
National Commission for Women
Deendayal Upadhyaya Marg
New Delhi - 110 002

Mr. V.K. Jain
National Commission for Women
Deendayal Upadhyaya Marg
New Delhi - 110 002

Ms. Gita Rana
National Commission for Women
Deendayal Upadhyaya Marg
New Delhi - 110 002

Ms. Padmaja Barua
National Commission for Women
Deendayal Upadhyaya Marg
New Delhi - 110 002

Ms. Jaganath
National Commission for Women
Deendayal Upadhyaya Marg
New Delhi - 110 002

Ms. Rita Panicker/Ms. Urmila Bendre
Butterflies Programme of Street and working Children
C-7, Ist Floor, Green Park Extension
New Delhi - 110 016

Dr. Subhalakshmi Subrahmanyam
Faculty Lady Irwin College
Sikandra Road, New Delhi

Ms. Sheila Sidhu
All India Women's Conference
6, Bhagwan Das Road
New Delhi - 110 001

Ms. Akshra Singh
Ladhy Irwin College
44, Satya Niketan, Moti Bagh-II
New Delhi

Ms. Rohini Sharma
Perspective Films
A2/37, SJE, III Floor
New Delhi - 110 029

Ms. Aloka Hiremath
Jamia Millia University
New Delhi

Mr. S.P. Thandi
NIPCCD
5, Institutional Area, Hauz Khas
New Delhi - 110 016

Dr. T. Kumar
Department of Women & Child
Government of India
Shastri Bhawan
New Delhi - 110 001

Ms. Pramila Dandavate
42, Meena Bagh
New Delhi

Ms. Anju
YWCA of India
10, Parliament Street
New Delhi - 110 001

Ms. Molly Joseph
Centre of Concern for Child Labour
P-40, Pandav Nagar
Mayur Vihar
New Delhi

Ms. Madhu Mathur
MUDRIT
D-33, Hauz Khas
New Delhi

Ms. Malati Chhibber
31, Prithviraj Road
New Delhi - 110 001

Ms. Lisa Vaughan
Reuters
Kautilya Marg
Delhi

Ms. Mudita Gupta
P.R.O. - National Commission for Women
Deendayal Upadhyaya Marg
New Delhi - 110 002

Ms. Asha Malik
P.A.O.- National Commission for Women
Deendayal Upadhyaya Marg
New Delhi - 110 002

Ms. Sunita Gadgil
President, Karuna
95, Sahajahan Road
New Delhi - 110 001

Mr. Khairatilal Bhola
22, Raja Garden
New Delhi

Ms. Diana Khambata
Guild of Service
C-25, Instt. Area, Behind Qutab Hotel
New Delhi

Ms. Leela Kasturi
CWDS
25, Bhai Vir Singh Marg
New Delhi - 110 001

Mr. Sweharan
C-4C/309, Janakpuri
New Delhi - 110 058

Mr. Vinod Arya
Advocate
19/1, Nizamuddin East
New Delhi - 110 013

Ms. Elizabeth Vatsyayan
AIDS Awareness Group

D-7, East of Kailash
New Delhi - 110 065

Mr. Siddhartha Vatsyayan
AIDS Awareness Group
D-7, East of Kailash
New Delhi - 110 065

Mr. Ranjan Roy
The Associated Press, U.S.A.

Mr. Bula
The Hindustan Time
K.G. Marg
New Delhi - 110 001

Ms. Darlina David
Christian Medical Association of India
2, A-3, Local Shopping Centre
Janakpuri
New Delhi - 110 058

Ms. Kalindi Thomas
Christian Medical Association of India
2, A-3, Local Shopping Centre
Janakpuri
New Delhi - 110 058

Ms. Shanti Mirza
Christian Medical Association of India
2, A-3, Local Shopping Centre
Janakpuri
New Delhi - 110 058

Ms. Rita Paul
Hope Project Charitable Trust
Nizamuddin Basti
New Delhi - 110 013

Ms. Kamla Nath
Centre for Social Research
C-4/68, S.D.A.
New Delhi - 110 016

Ms. Maria Mangte
Tribal Welfare Society
New Delhi

Mr. A. Bhandare
ANKUR
7/10, Sarvapriya Vihar
New Delhi

Ms. Alok Srivastav
YAAR
323/B, J&K Pocket
Dilshad Garden
Delhi - 110 095

Ms. Karoline Davis
Indian Social Institute
10, Institutional Area,
Lodhi Road
New Delhi - 110 003

Sr. Shalini SCN
Indian Social Institute
10, Institutional Area
Lodhi Road
New Delhi - 110 003

Ms. Sarla Mudgal
Kalyani
5030 Kalidas Marg
Darya Ganj
New Delhi

Mr. S.K. Bhalla
Kalyani
5030 Kalidas Marg
Darya Ganj
New Delhi

Ms. Meera Asthana
YWCA of Delhi
1 Ashok Road
New Delhi - 110 001

Ms. Rosie Mathews
YWCA of Delhi
1 Ashok Road
New Delhi - 110 001

Ms. Hazel Samuel
AIACHE
Lokbodhan Kendra
36, Institutional Area
Pankha Road, D-Block
Janakpuri
New Delhi - 110 036

Ms. Neelam Dang
CHELSEA
207/Sector 29
Noida

Ms. Anu Singh
CHELSEA
207/Sector 29
Noida

Mr. Surendar Saini
Delhi Social Welfare Advisory Board
New Delhi

Dr. Asha Chandra
41, North Avenue
New Delhi

Mr. Charan Singh
Bharat Vikas Parishad
Janakpuri Branch
New Delhi - 110 058

Ms. Divya Malik
Reporter - New Delhi Television
New Delhi

Dr. Klaus Voll
Journalist
B-3, Nizamuddin East
New Delhi - 110 013

Ms. Molly Joseph
Centre of Concern for Child Labour
P-40/A, 1st Floor, Pandav Nagar
Mayur Vihar Phase-I
Delhi - 110 092

Ms. Pramila Dandavate
42, Meena Bagh
New Delhi

Mr. Surendra Prakash
Ward No. III
House No.682 (Near Roopanwala Kuon)
Mehrauli
New Delhi - 110 030

Ms. Suraiya Durrany
Hayat Centre for Education
Research and Action
B-72 Mohan Gardens
New Delhi - 110 059

Ms. Puneeta Roy
Perspective Films
A-1/25, Safdarjung Development Area
New Delhi - 110 001

Mr. Chaman Gautam
Danik Jagran
New Delhi

Ms. Vimla Vohra
Member-in-Charge - Bapnu Ghar
All India Women's Conference
6, Bhagwan Das Road, New Delhi - 110 001

Ms. Aalvers R.
UNIFEM
55, Lodi Estate
New Delhi - 110 003

Ms. Veena Samuel
Joint Women's Programme
14 Jangpura-B,
New Delhi - 110 014.

Ms. Lalitha S.A.
Joint Women's Programme
14 Jangpura B
New Delhi - 110 014

Ms. Madhu Joshi
Joint Women's Programme
14 Jangpura B
New Delhi - 110 014

Ms. Vinita Thomas
Joint Women's Programme
14 Jangpura B
New Delhi - 110 014

Ms. Upala Devi
ANWIC
14 Jangpura B
New Delhi - 110 014